The PBIS Tier Three Handbook

The PBIS Tier Three Handbook

A Practical Guide to Implementing Individualized Interventions

Jessica Djabrayan Hannigan and John E. Hannigan

CORWIN

A SAGE Publishing Company

FOR INFORMATION:

Corwin

A SAGE Company

2455 Teller Road

Thousand Oaks, California 91320

(800) 233-9936

www.corwin.com

SAGE Publications Ltd.

1 Oliver's Yard

55 City Road

London EC1Y 1SP

United Kingdom

SAGE Publications India Pvt. Ltd.

B 1/I 1 Mohan Cooperative Industrial Area

Mathura Road, New Delhi 110 044

India

SAGE Publications Asia-Pacific Pte. Ltd.

3 Church Street

#10-04 Samsung Hub

Singapore 049483

Program Director: Jessica Allan

Associate Editor: Lucas Schleicher

Editorial Assistant: Mia Rodriguez

Production Editor: Tori Mirsadjadi

Copy Editor: Melinda Masson

Typesetter: C&M Digitals (P) Ltd.

Proofreader: Gretchen Treadwell

Indexer: Maria Sosnowski

Cover Designer: Michael Dubowe

Marketing Manager: Charline Maher

Printed in the United States of America

Library of Congress Cataloging-in-Publication Data

Names: Djabrayan Hannigan, Jessica, author. | Hannigan, John E., author.

Title: The PBIS tier three handbook : a practical guide to implementing individualized interventions / Jessica Djabrayan Hannigan and John E. Hannigan.

Description: Thousand Oaks, California : Corwin, 2018. | Includes index.

Identifiers: LCCN 2017060059 | ISBN 9781544301174 (pbk. : alk. paper)

Subjects: LCSH: School psychology—United States. | Behavior modification—United States. | School children—United States—Discipline. | Students—United States—Psychology. | School management and organization—United States.

Classification: LCC LB1060.2 .D54 2018 | DDC 371.39/3—dc23

LC record available at https://lccn.loc.gov/2017060059

This book is printed on acid-free paper.

MIX
Paper from responsible sources
FSC www.fsc.org FSC® C008955

19 20 21 22 10 9 8 7 6 5 4 3

Contents

Preface

We wrote *The PBIS Tier Three Handbook* to accompany and extend the work of *The PBIS Tier One Handbook* and *The PBIS Tier Two Handbook* published by Corwin. *The PBIS Tier One Handbook* provides a framework with practical steps for implementation for schools and districts establishing a Tier 1 (School-Wide) behavior system. *The PBIS Tier Two Handbook* is framed to serve a similar purpose for implementing a Tier 2 (Targeted/At-Risk) behavior system. *The PBIS Tier Three Handbook* is designed to provide a similar frame for implementing a Tier 3 (Individualized) behavior system. It will give the user a step-by-step framework based on effective implementation of Tier 3 interventions for both general education and special education students. This book includes practical examples, case scenarios, and rubrics for identifying current states of implementation with tips to close gaps from recommended actions and examples. This book will also be used in teacher, support services, and administrator preparation programs and for training and professional development purposes for educators, service providers, and school- and district-level administrators. The series of PBIS handbooks (1, 2, and 3) is designed to be interactive in nature.

CRITICAL TAKEAWAYS

This book is designed to help you, as an educator, achieve three things at your school:

1. Build on the Tier 1 and Tier 2 behavior systems of your school

2. Create a Tier 3 behavior response system with procedures and protocols that address individualized behavior needs for both general education and special education students

3. Develop and implement Tier 3 interventions within this Tier 3 system based on student needs and data

> ### Note
>
> You need all three tiers in place to achieve sustainable behavioral outcomes at your school. The ultimate goal is to develop a tiered behavior system designed to respond to student social-emotional needs at each level of intensity by adding additional layers of support. We often work with schools that have difficulty in both the general education and special education contexts serving students who need Tier 3 intensive interventions. Often, we get asked, what do we do? Sometimes this is difficult for us to answer because for students needing Tier 3 interventions, it is not a one-size-fits-all approach. In fact, most of the case studies and research in this area provide case study examples for how to respond to students who need this level of support.

This book will ensure you have established a Tier 3 system that will support your school's Tier 3 intervention needs, and will serve as a guide to reflect on your current practices and enhance them to attain the best outcomes for students who need additional supports beyond Tier 1 and Tier 2.

About the Authors

Dr. Jessica Djabrayan Hannigan is an assistant professor in the Educational Leadership Department at California State University, Fresno. She has extensive experience in P–12 general education and special education administration at the school and district level. She also works as an educational consultant, training approximately 500 schools across the country on implementing effective and equitable academic and behavior systems in schools and districts. She currently serves as a member of the Center for Leadership, Equity, and Research (CLEAR) and the Fix School Discipline Coalition.

Dr. John E. Hannigan is principal of Reagan Elementary in the Sanger Unified School District in California. He has served in education for 15 years as a principal, assistant principal, instructional coach, and teacher. Dr. Hannigan specializes in building strong school cultures, developing leaders at all levels, and creating effective academic and behavior systems. Under his leadership, his school has received numerous awards and recognitions, including California State Distinguished School, Gold Ribbon School, Title I Academic School, and Positive Behavioral Interventions and

Supports (gold level), and has been recognized as an exemplary Response to Intervention (RTI) school for both academics and behavior. His school was selected as a knowledge development site for the statewide scaling up of Multi-Tiered Systems of Support (MTSS). He currently serves as a member of the Center for Leadership, Equity, and Research (CLEAR).

Before You Begin:

How to Use *The PBIS Tier Three Handbook*

The Why: A strong need exists for schools to build social-emotional systems to respond to students demonstrating intensive individualized behavioral needs.

The What: *The PBIS Tier Three Handbook* is a framework designed for educators to create a Tier 3 system that incorporates Tier 3 interventions for students in need of individualized behavior interventions.

The How: Educators learn how to implement the ABCs of Tier 3. Practical examples and guidance are provided to create a system that fits their school's needs.

WHAT IS THIS BOOK DESIGNED TO HELP YOU DO?

This book is designed to help you, as an educator, continue the development of tiered behavior systems in your school or district. Specifically, this book focuses on designing a system that responds to Tier 3 behavior intervention needs. So . . . What does this look like? What does it sound like? How will we know if the Tier 3 interventions are working? The intended outcome for the development of this book is for you to use this frame to guide the implementation of effective Tier 3 interventions tailored to fit your individual school's needs.

In working with a large number of schools, we have identified that if the Tier 3 system is not in place to support general education and special education students demonstrating these needs, the culture of the school is diminished. A positive school culture will never be created without its teachers on board. Unless teachers are supported by championing students' ability to succeed and ensuring students feel appreciated, the culture will begin to crack. Teachers have a difficult job—one that requires them daily to develop both the academic and social-emotional well-being of students, with some requiring more time than others. When teachers are not given the proper supports to help their students with the most intensive challenges, they will begin to feel resentment toward their administration and/or vexation toward their students.

For the purpose of this book, we are referring to students in need of a Tier 3 behavior response (most intensive; both general education and special education in your school). When we say *Tier 3 response*, we are referencing, but not limiting it to, students on medication for behavior, students not properly medicated, students requiring constant attention and multiple staff to stabilize, students with intensive behavior plans, students not responding to Tier 1 or 2 supports, and students transitioned into a general education classroom from alternative education without proper interventions and supports in place.

Consider a hospital intensive care unit: if an individual needs this level of intensive health support, he or she receives an individualized health intervention or plan that is timely and based on medical history, previously attempted interventions, and more. This is similar to a child who needs intensive supports with an individualized behavior plan to improve his or her behavior in school. It cannot be a one-size-fits-all intervention approach; each child who needs this level of support needs an individualized plan based on his or her needs.

If adequate support is not put in place to address this small percentage of students in schools, struggling teachers will soon make their voices heard. Some examples are on the opposite page.

Comments from teachers struggling with how to respond to students who need Tier 3 interventions

I can't control him/her.

He/She comes in screaming and does not do anything in my class.

I feel like I am so weak and have no control over my class when he/she is at school.

I feel like I am a bad teacher.

It feels like it is something I am doing that triggers him/her.

I take his/her behavior personally even though I know I am not supposed to.

I started using my personal and sick days for the first time in my career because I cannot handle the stress.

I do not receive adequate supports from the administrator or special education teacher/staff.

Having a student that intense with no help makes me want to stay home from school.

I feel depressed when I think about coming to work.

I gave myself a panic attack the other day because he/she was so challenging.

It is the first time in my career I feel as if I need my union representative to help.

I feel like my administrators are blaming me for his/her behavior.

The student runs out of my class whenever he/she wants and is escorted back by an administrator.

I start to get frustrated and can't think.

I feel lightheaded and blank when he/she takes over my class.

I don't know what to do anymore.

The behavior plan is too complex and hard to implement without support.

The administrator just brings him/her back without any action or explanation.

The school psychologist does a drive-by observation anytime I ask for support.

The counselor told me his/her caseload is too full to help.

The parents make comments to me that he/she never had behavior issues before my class although school records show differently.

It is not safe for the other students.

Everyone knows how bad he/she is at the school.

My administrator is not documenting any of the behaviors.

I am burned out.

I am at the point where I just ignore him/her and call the office at least three times a day.

No one knows what to do with him/her.

He/She is running our school.

I feel so alone.

I feel like his/her behavior is going to be reflected on my teacher evaluations.

I am trying everything the support staff tells me, but it is not working.

My class can learn when he/she is not here.

The parents are not supportive.

Here are some ways you can HELP teachers in these cases.

H—Hear the teacher out. Teachers need to feel safe to share with their administrators when they need help. Teachers who truly care about students will try every strategy in their arsenal to support a student before involving the administration. This is a stark difference from the teacher who calls the office about everything. When teachers who rarely do so finally ask for help, it should be regarded as a top priority to help them. Teachers take misbehavior to heart, especially when a student doesn't respond to a behavior intervention that worked in the past with a previous student. They feel bad asking for help and burdening others and see it as a negative reflection of their professional ability if they request support, which, of course, couldn't be further from the truth.

E—Evaluate how you can support instead of placing all of the responsibility on the teacher. As the administrator or support provider, take time to research everything about the student. For example, read the student's cumulative file, call the previous school or placement, talk to teachers who have worked with the student, talk to the parents, review the special education file if applicable, and so on. Unfortunately, at times, an administrator or support provider will respond to a teacher's request for help by "showing support" through a onetime twenty- to twenty-five-minute observation indicating areas in which the teacher needs to focus attention. This is not a sufficient response and is condescending to the teacher. Additionally, without the context of the entire situation, the observation feedback will not be effective. One "drive-by" observation is not credible and weak at best.

L—Learn about behaviors, functions, and triggers. Most teachers are not trained to respond to extreme behaviors. Most can handle basic daily student misbehavior, but many have not learned how to adequately respond to students needing Tier 3 intensive supports. For example, updating a behavior support plan or creating a plan without proper assistance for Tier 3 behaviors is not a recommended approach (and could put the teacher in a liable situation when dealing with a student on an Individualized Education Program); we have actually seen this happen in schools. We then wonder why the teacher has not bought in or why the plan does not work. If you want a teacher to learn how to work with students in need of this level of support, then as the administrator or support provider, ensure you know how to do so as well. A student requiring this level of support will require a team approach.

P—Plan an appropriate response to the behavior collaboratively with all stakeholders. The plan and response need to be timely and practical for all. Unfortunately, school teams often wait until the behavior has reached an unmanageable level and relationships have been fractured. Teachers need to feel safe and supported. A Tier 3 level of behavior needs a Tier 3 level of stakeholder support. A teacher cannot do it alone. So, stop asking good teachers who have a genuine need for support to implement unrealistic plans alone with no support. It is damaging to the morale of the teacher and the culture of the school when this is the approach from the administration. Additionally, imagine the angst of teachers in future grade levels worrying about the impending placement of this student, knowing they will be left to manage these behaviors alone without supportive leadership.

Note

Use the acronym HELP to assess whether or not you are helping teachers in cases where they are working with the most challenging students in your school. Establishing a tiered behavior response system like the one in this book and our previous books will help you minimize these feelings from teachers and staff and allow you to maintain the buy-in to continue implementation. Keep this HELP acronym in mind as you are developing and implementing the markers, characteristics, and SMART goals in this book.

Date: _____ Teacher Needing Support: _____ Student Name: _____

PBIS Tier 3 Sub-Team Members: _____

H (Hear)	*E* (Evaluate)	*L* (Learn)	*P* (Plan)

We really empathize with the many great teachers out there who are not receiving adequate support when working with Tier 3 behaviors in their classrooms. They need HELP, and administrators and support providers need to work closely with them in these cases. However, when administrators and support providers don't know how to provide adequate help and support for this level of behavior, it is a perfect storm of nonintervention. A system designed to help teachers respond is needed in these instances. Use *The PBIS Tier One Handbook*, *The PBIS Tier Two Handbook*, and *Don't Suspend Me!* to help create systems that support behaviors at all levels.

However, this HELP model is not the typical response for students who struggle with their behavior. Without critical markers and characteristics in place, such as the few mentioned in this section, you have work to do in creating, refining, and sustaining effective Tier 3 behavior systems at your school or district. This book is designed to build on the foundation of the Tier 1 and Tier 2 PBIS handbooks and (1) create a system to respond to Tier 3 behavior intervention needs, (2) help Tier 3 behavior teams identify individualized behavior intervention needs of the school, (3) help Tier 3 behavior teams establish individualized behavior interventions with all critical markers and characteristics in place, and (4) implement and monitor with fidelity the Tier 3 intervention SMART goals.

We also want to intentionally note that this book is designed to help educators with the Tier 3 system at their school no matter what programs or initiatives they prefer to implement. This book is also designed to make sure a process is in place to monitor and adjust effectiveness of interventions and implementation. This book is written by practitioners for practitioners. We want to provide a resource not only to educate educators on methods to address intensive individualized needs of a school, but also to help them learn from effective, practical leaders who have been successful in implementing responses that work to help stabilize students in need while balancing the emotional drain of serving in that role.

Our framework is referred to as the PBIS Champion Model; however, we want to emphasize this does not mean our frame does not have the flexibility to include other effective programs and initiatives as part of the tiered system we are helping educators design. In fact, we highly recommend the use of best practices. Our goal is to help you evaluate, organize, and refine your systems in a method that can be sustainable and replicable for other schools and districts. We are not in competition with other initiatives. What makes this framework unique is that we encourage the use of other programs and interventions that help you meet your school behavior goals. We understand some PBIS models do not allow for an interconnection of initiatives, which makes the Champion Model a unique vehicle to help connect and enhance existing and new initiatives based on your desired outcomes for *all* students.

This book encourages a collaborative and practical approach to designing and monitoring Tier 3 behavior interventions. On the following pages we have compiled the most commonly asked questions and answers as you begin designing a school system that responds to individualized behaviors of students.

FREQUENTLY ASKED QUESTIONS

What is a Tier 3 intervention?

A Tier 3 intervention is designed to meet students' individualized needs based on the function of their behavior. A Tier 3 intervention occurs in addition to the Tier 1 and Tier 2 interventions offered at the school. Students needing a Tier 3 intervention require a more intensive level of support with one or two behaviors being explicitly addressed at a time. If following the tiered system of behavioral response, there should only be a minimal number of students at your school needing a Tier 3 intervention— approximately 1 to 5 percent of the school (note that this is only the case if your school has strong Tier 1 and Tier 2 systems in place).

Are Tier 3 interventions only for special education students?

Tier 3 interventions are not necessarily only for special education students although we do consider any student in need of a special education behavior support plan as a student needing Tier 3 structures and supports. Some special education students may be responding to their behavior support plan but need it in place to maintain that level of behavior; therefore, we always include special education students with behavior support plans in our school's Tier 3 intervention count. However, general education students may also need a structured, individualized plan of behavior support but may not be in the special education realm.

How long does a student need to be in Tier 2 before moving to Tier 3?

Students transitioning to Tier 3 need to be decided on a case-by-case basis by the Tier 2 and Tier 3 sub-team. However, usually it is recommended that a student receive an appropriate Tier 2 intervention for at least six to eight weeks with fidelity before effectiveness is decided. Also, sometimes a student might need to try another Tier 2 intervention or a combination of interventions prior to considering the Tier 3 level of supports. Note: If a student escalates quickly and needs a more intensive level of supports, there is no rule saying students cannot be immediately moved to Tier 3. In this book, you will learn the role of the PBIS Tier 2 and Tier 3 sub-team members and how they use data and criteria to move students to the next level of intensive supports as a collaborative team.

Do students have to go through Tier 2 before being put into a Tier 3 intervention?

Students do not always receive Tier 2 intervention ahead of Tier 3. Sometimes students who need a Tier 3 level of support enroll in our schools, or a student may experience trauma or another significant event that may trigger intense behaviors; in these cases, it is critical to provide the appropriate level of response right away in order to stabilize the students' behavior and thus give them access to their education. In these cases, it is critical to really understand the context or contact their previous schools if possible to learn everything you can to help develop an appropriate Tier 3 intervention for these students.

How long do I progress monitor a student before determining that the student isn't responding to the Tier 3 intervention?

Individualized Tier 3 interventions are challenging to implement and monitor. Again, it is critical that we remember it is called an individualized intervention for a reason—no one child is the same. For students on a special education Tier 3 behavior plan, there are some built-in frames for progress monitoring behavior support plan goals and meetings with parents and stakeholders to discuss progress. However, although this structure is in place, it is not always utilized with fidelity as it should be. General education students do not have a formal document aligned with federal law for their Tier 3 intervention; thus, these interventions are just as important and also need some form of structure to monitor and evaluate effectiveness. In general, the Tier 3 sub-team should discuss all students on a Tier 3 intervention, both general education and special education, on at least a weekly basis with the use of data to decide if they are responding or not. This should include a process for gathering feedback from all the stakeholders on fidelity of implementation and effectiveness prior to making additional decisions. Often, Tier 3 interventions will need to be refined, and goals for progress will need to be set, taking into consideration the seriousness of the behavior. For example, these goals should be set up for student success (e.g., "Student A will meet all his behavior goals 80 percent of the time" would not be ideal for a student needing this intense of an intervention). A student's goal should be realistic and focused on one or two behaviors at a time with ample opportunities for teaching, generalization, and practice. So to answer the question, as a Tier 3 sub-team, you can decide if a Tier 3 intervention is not working after also evaluating the realistic expectations. Usually, we suggest a ten-day intensive implementation of a Tier 3 intervention with fidelity utilizing all resources before deciding effectiveness or not.

Who implements the Tier 3 interventions?

Implementation depends on the Tier 3 intervention plan. The most effective Tier 3 interventions are delivered in a collaborative, team approach for effectiveness. You will learn about the process of conducting a Tier 3 human resource and stakeholder inventory in the book, and it will help you decide who should be part of implementing each Tier 3 intervention plan.

How can I create fidelity buy-in with a teacher who says, "I've tried it, and it doesn't work" after only implementing the intervention for a few days?

First of all, creating buy-in goes back to how well the culture of tiered behavior supports is established at your school. It is important to make the connection between how teachers are expected to respond to students having academic difficulties and how administrators and support staff are expected to respond to teachers having students who demonstrate intensive behavior difficulties. So setting up your expectation for what is expected from the staff at the school comes first; however, there are many cases where really good teachers who also have good belief systems feel frustrated. When you start to hear comments similar to "I've tried it, and it doesn't work," this is a reflection of teachers being made to feel like the Tier 3 intervention is not a team approach. If that is how a teacher feels, then the Tier 3 intervention will fail on multiple levels.

What if the students are not taking their medication?

Medication is always a touchy subject because there is only so much we can do at the school level. However, establishing a relationship with parents or guardians and getting a release of information signed for the school to be allowed to also communicate with prescribing doctors have worked wonders for us. For example, in one case, a student would escalate very quickly on days he did not have his medication. So connecting with the doctor and getting proper permissions to have extra medication at the school in the nurse's office in case the student missed a dose made a huge difference for him.

How do I help teachers recognize that a student is making progress when they are only focused on the negative behaviors still occurring?

It is important again to set idealistic goals and visit students' progress with the direct stakeholders. Sometimes, teachers feel like it is their fault if a student is not making progress at the speed that they expect. When others (e.g., administrators or support providers) make comments that the student is improving there needs to be a collective definition of what "improving" means. Without the teacher's input, this could lead to teacher resentment and continued focus on the negative behaviors.

What if the rest of the staff thinks that a student on a Tier 3 intervention is running the school?

It is important for administrators to have a professional conversation with their staff on the meaning of a Tier 3 intervention. If staff members are not aware that students receiving this level of intervention have supports, they are going to establish misconceptions about these students and how the administration is responding. Note: This does not mean confidential information about students' private records needs to be shared; it just means that the stakeholders articulate to the rest of the staff that they are working together as a team to help these students get to a stable place where they can access their education.

⁂

What are some questions you may have before you delve into the next section of this book?

_____

_____

_____

_____

_____

_____

_____

_____

_____

Part I
Overview

The PBIS Champion Model

In *The PBIS Tier One Handbook*, your team learned how to establish the Tier 1 foundation at your school. *The PBIS Tier Two Handbook* helped you learn how to establish a system that allows for effective Tier 2 interventions to be offered based on the data and needs of the students at your school. In this book, the Tier 3 component of the PBIS Champion Model will be reviewed. This book is unique in that there is not a one-size-fits-all approach for students who need a Tier 3 behavior intervention. However, as stated in the previous books, students' behavioral needs should be addressed with the same level of focus and attention as their academic needs. In this case, the individualized behavior needs of a student should be addressed similar to an individualized approach to academic support. If the "School-Wide" and "Targeted/At-Risk" behavior supports you learned how to provide do not work for students needing additional intervention, it is time to consider an individualized approach.

So to review, the PBIS Champion Model is a comprehensive systems approach for the design and delivery of Positive Behavior Interventions and Supports (PBIS) in a school. This action-oriented framework provides *quality criteria* and *how-to steps* for developing, implementing, monitoring, and sustaining each level of the system: Bronze (Tier 1), Silver (Tier 2), and Gold (Tier 3). Each tier in the system consists of three categories: Category A—Markers, Category B—Characteristics, and Category C—Academic and Behavior Goals and the Work of the PBIS Team. Each category is composed

Figure 1.1

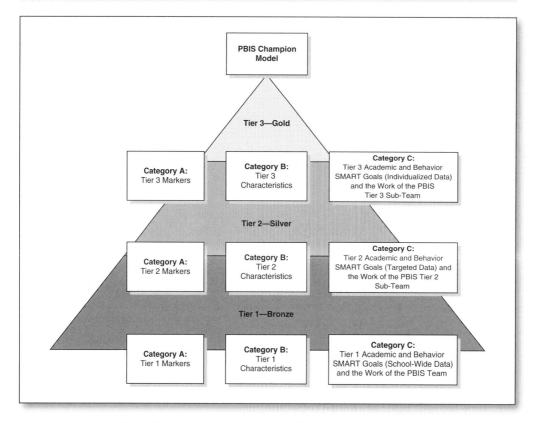

of quality criteria and a set of defined actions. Figure 1.1 provides a brief overview of the quality criteria for each tier with a quick glimpse of what a Champion Model School looks like at each level (Bronze, Silver, and Gold).

In order to attain and sustain the Gold Level implementation at your school, it is essential that you continue meeting the goals for Tier 1 and Tier 2 implementation. Usually, establishing an entire behavior system at a school takes three to five years, so do not be hard on yourself as this work begins to get challenging. For example, throughout your work in establishing this model, you will receive pushback from some who do not believe in *all* students.

The individualized approach tends to be met with more frustration by stakeholders due to the amount of energy and time it takes to help students in need of this level of support. Time after time we run into teachers with a very negative view toward how administration responds to students with intensive needs. Because of the aforementioned ineffective implementation, the failure of PBIS ultimately gets blamed on the entire system, rather than its implementation. If all ten markers in *The PBIS Tier One Handbook* and all eight markers in *The PBIS Tier Two Handbook* are not in place, you are not doing PBIS, and you are definitely not going to have a system in place that will allow for a proper response to a student's need for intensive individualized interventions.

Also, don't get caught up with the semantics; call it what you want—Response to Intervention (RTI) behavior or Multi-Tiered System of Supports (MTSS) behavior—but the fact remains: Do you have a system of multi-increasingly intensive tiers of support for students who struggle with their behavior? The PBIS Champion Model, as a framework, is designed to help educators work together through a problem-solving model to provide an equitable education, support academic and behavior needs in a systematic way that addresses the needs of *all* students, and aligns the entire system of initiatives, supports, and resources while implementing continuous improvement processes across all levels of the system. From our experience, most school administrators and staff indicate their school has some degree of a system in place to reactively respond to a student's Tier 3 behavior challenges, but many concede that they struggle with implementing effective Tier 3 interventions. The PBIS Champion Model will help you gather baseline information and provide criteria for establishing effective tiered systems in your school.

So how do we do this in our schools? Where do we start? How do we strengthen our implementation of existing systems to address all of these components?

You will need to assess your Tier 3 intervention system's current state prior to beginning this work. Most decisions within this level of the PBIS Champion Model are made by the PBIS Tier 3 sub-team; this team can be an expansion of the PBIS Tier 2 sub-team. In order to assess your current state and to ensure coherence throughout your system, begin by answering the following questions.

❦❦

What is the number of students currently on a special education behavior support plan at your school?

_____

_____

_____

(Continued)

(Continued)

Can you articulate the behavior support plan steps to take in case you need to help with a Tier 3 response?

_____

_____

_____

Do you believe that all the stakeholders involved with the implementation of the behavior support plan know the exact steps to prevent or respond if a student's behavior escalates?

_____

_____

_____

How did you do? Usually, we find that a school psychologist or possibly an administrator can answer one or more of these questions, but the rest of the sub-team or the stakeholders aligned with the behavior support plan will not feel confident in their response. This is an indicator that currently your school has a reactive system in place for responding to students with Tier 3 intervention needs, rather than a proactive system in place; hence, the goal of this book is to help you establish and tighten these systems so you will know all students at your school who are currently on an individualized plan, whether or not they are responding, whether or not the implementation of the plan is happening with fidelity, and how-to steps to take when you have other students who are in need of an intensive individualized behavior plan.

We recommend you start by completing the following "Tier 3 Supports at a Glance" section prior to beginning this work. This will help you identify the individual students who are currently receiving Tier 3 interventions and, based on the total enrollment of students at your school, the percentage of students who are on a Tier 3 intervention at this time.

TIER 3 SUPPORTS AT A GLANCE

What is the total number of students enrolled at your school?	
How many special education students on your campus have a behavior support plan in place (connected to an Individualized Education Program, or IEP)?	
How many general education students on your campus have a general education Tier 3 behavior support plan in place?	
What is the percentage of students on a Tier 3 behavior support plan at your school (general education and special education combined total divided by total number of students enrolled at the school = percentage of students on a Tier 3 intervention)?	

Note: *No more than 1 to 5 percent of students at the school should be receiving a Tier 3 intervention.*

TIER 3 SUPPORTS: STUDENT DATA DRILL-DOWN

Student Name	Grade	Special Education or General Education	Reason for Behavior Support Plan	Do all stakeholders know their role with the plan?

━━━━━━━━━━━━━━━━━━━━ ❧❧ ━━━━━━━━━━━━━━━━━━━━

If you were **able** to assess the percentage of students receiving a Tier 3 behavior intervention at your school, what percentage did you get? What are your next steps? What are some questions you may have?

_____

_____

_____

_____

_____

If you were **unable** to assess the percentage of students receiving a Tier 3 behavior intervention at your school, what are your next steps to gather this information? What are some questions you may have?

_____

_____

_____

_____

_____

━━━━━━━━━━━━━━━━━━━━ ❧❧ ━━━━━━━━━━━━━━━━━━━━

In the next chapter, you will begin to learn about the Tier 3 system aligned with the Champion Model Gold Level.

The What and Why of a PBIS Tier 3 System

Creating effective behavior systems in schools requires multiple layers of supports and maneuvering around complex systems. The majority of students will respond to a solid Tier 1 (School-Wide) behavior system (see *The PBIS Tier One Handbook*); however, some students will require Tier 2 (Targeted/At-Risk) behavior interventions (see *The PBIS Tier Two Handbook*), and a smaller percentage will require a Tier 3 (Individualized) intervention/response in order to access their education.

Students who meet a set of criteria for individualized interventions (meaning Tier 1 and Tier 2 systems are in place with fidelity but the individual student is not responding) need to have additional opportunities based on the function of their behavior to learn the appropriate ways to behave. A Tier 3 intervention is commonly defined as an intervention for students who require an intensive/individualized response in order to stabilize their behavior. Approximately 1 to 5 percent of the students in your school may need some level of a Tier 3 intervention. This definition alone does not break down the complex criteria and steps necessary for creating, implementing, and monitoring an effective Tier 3 intervention/response—hence, the purpose of the PBIS Champion Model Gold Level Framework. This model can be seen in Figure 2.1 on the next page.

Figure 2.1

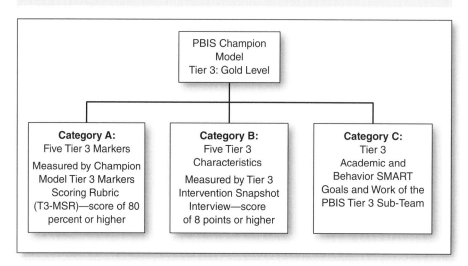

So how would administration and staff react to a student needing a Tier 3 intervention at a Gold Level PBIS Champion Model School? Based on your current knowledge, does School Environment A or School Environment B represent a Gold Level PBIS Champion Model School? Which school would you prefer to be a part of?

School Environment A	School Environment B
When School A's administration and staff receive notification that a new student with extreme behavioral challenges is going to enroll in their school from a neighboring school for a "fresh start," they roll up their sleeves and are ready to provide all the individualized help the student needs to succeed at the school.	When School B's administration and staff receive notification that a new student with extreme behavioral challenges is going to enroll in their school from a neighboring school for a "fresh start," they complain, advocate to keep the student in the other school, are stressed out about where to place the student, and blame this decision on the district office.

What school did you select? How would your school administration and staff currently respond given the same scenario?

_____

_____

_____

_____

_____

A PBIS Champion Model School's administration and staff would respond similar to School Environment A. In addition to this type of supportive and "ready to do whatever it takes" culture at a Gold Level school, you would see evidence of the critical Tier 3 markers, characteristics, and established academic and behavior SMART goals—or goals that are Strategic and Specific, Measurable, Attainable/Achievable, Results-Oriented and Relevant, and Time-Bound—with data evidencing progress and effectiveness of Tier 3 interventions at your school.

Tier 3
Markers

Marker 1: Establish and Operate an Effective PBIS Tier 3 Sub-Team
Marker 2: Establish a Culture and Expectation for Supporting All Students
Marker 3: Conduct a Tier 3 Resource Inventory
Marker 4: Establish a Tier 3 Timely Response Plan
Marker 5: Establish a Tier 3 Fidelity Check Process

Tier 3
Characteristics

Characteristic 1: Conduct a Student History Review
Characteristic 2: Conduct an Environment Review
Characteristic 3: Identify Function and Provide Replacement Skills
Characteristic 4: Present Evidence of a Practical Plan/Schedule
Characteristic 5: Plan for Progress Monitoring/Communication

Tier 3
Academic and Behavior SMART Goals

SMART Goal Academic: A Tier 3 academic goal is an individualized intervention academic SMART goal drafted by the PBIS Tier 3 sub-team and other stakeholders based on individualized academic data of the student receiving the Tier 3 intervention at the school.

SMART Goal Behavior: A Tier 3 behavior goal is an individualized intervention behavior SMART goal drafted by the PBIS Tier 3 sub-team and other stakeholders based on individualized behavior data of the student receiving the Tier 3 intervention at the school.

How to establish a PBIS Champion Model Gold Level school is outlined in the next chapters. **As you begin this journey, please make sure to continue referring to the critical takeaways of this book:** *Build on the Tier 1 and Tier 2 behavior system of your school, Create a Tier 3 behavior response system with procedures and protocols in place to address individualized behavior needs (addresses approximately 1 to 5 percent of students in a tiered behavior system both in special education and in general education), and develop and implement Tier 3 interventions in an individualized fashion based on the function or perceived function of behavior.*

Part II

The PBIS Tier Three Handbook

Getting Started With Category A— Tier 3 Markers

This chapter identifies and describes the Tier 3 markers of a Gold Level Positive Behavior Interventions and Supports (PBIS) Champion Model, explains how to assess your system's current state relative to each marker, presents some challenges real schools face and approaches to address those challenges, and provides detailed lists of actions for moving your system toward its desired future as a Gold Level PBIS Champion Model. The intent of this chapter is to help you build a system designed to support the effective delivery of Tier 3 interventions at your school.

Note

The Tier 3 markers identified in this chapter are designed to build on the Tier 1 and Tier 2 system markers, so it is essential that they are also put in place with fidelity first. It is also important to note that this book was written for practitioners by practitioners who have extensive background in both general education and special education systems. As practitioners, we know the difficulty of responding to Tier 3–level behaviors; therefore, we wanted to provide a resource for you that was thorough yet practical in nature.

What is a Tier 3 behavior system? A Tier 3 behavior system at a school is designed to support 1 to 5 percent of the school's population. Typically, Tier 3 interventions are provided to students demonstrating intensive/individualized behavior needs. The ultimate goal is to identify the function (the why, the triggers, the antecedents, etc.) of the behavior and to stabilize students' behavior so they can access their education. Students needing this intensive level of support may also be receiving special education services. Often these students need to learn specific individualized skills, strategies, or replacement behaviors tailored to their social-emotional needs. This chapter will help you identify any gaps in developing such a system. If more than 1 to 5 percent of the total student body needs Tier 3 interventions at your school, it is highly recommended that you revisit your school-wide foundation (see *The PBIS Tier One Handbook*) and targeted intervention system (see *The PBIS Tier Two Handbook*).

CRITICAL TAKEAWAYS

- In this chapter, you will learn how to implement the five markers essential for building a Tier 3 behavior system at your school. By *Tier 3 behavior system*, we mean the big-picture lens of how your school responds to students needing Tier 3 interventions. Is there a response that is timely, with needed resources? Implementing all five Tier 3 markers with fidelity will help you create an effective and sustainable Tier 3 behavior system designed to support the Tier 3 interventions offered at your school; you will learn how to establish and implement Tier 3 interventions in Chapter 4.
- Without a frame to support implementation, monitoring, and communication of the offered Tier 3 interventions at your school, they will not work.
- In this chapter, you will find criteria and examples of evidence for each marker. To avoid getting overwhelmed, select one or two actions at a time and make sure they are implemented with fidelity.
- Use a systematic lens of the school as you navigate through each marker in this chapter. In this chapter, the focus is on creating the big-picture system, and in Chapter 4, the focus will be on what a Tier 3 intervention should include in order to be effective for students. Without the big-picture system, the effectiveness of Tier 3 interventions will be minimal.
- Remember, the five Tier 3 markers highlighted in this chapter are designed to build on the markers identified in Tier 1 and Tier 2. You will see some markers in this chapter that may overlap with some markers you implemented in *The PBIS Tier Two Handbook*. That is exactly what this book is designed to do: help you add to previously implemented markers and expand implementation to include Tier 3 components.

So what are the Tier 3 markers of a Gold Level PBIS Champion Model?

In order to build a strong Tier 3 behavior response system, five critical markers must be in place:

Marker 1: Establish and Operate an Effective PBIS Tier 3 Sub-Team

Marker 2: Establish a Culture and Expectation for Supporting All Students

Marker 3: Conduct a Tier 3 Resource Inventory

Marker 4: Establish a Tier 3 Timely Response Plan

Marker 5: Establish a Tier 3 Fidelity Check Process

These five Tier 3 markers can be assessed through the Tier 3 Markers Scoring Rubric (T3-MSR), used to help a school establish a Tier 3 behavior system implementation baseline and recognized as a valid tool to measure and monitor progress of implementing PBIS Tier 3 markers in schools. A complete T3-MSR can be found at the end of this chapter. The indicator evidencing a strong Tier 3 behavior system foundation in alignment with the Gold PBIS Champion Model is an overall **T3-MSR score of 80 percent or higher, which is equivalent to 24 points or more out of a total 30 points.**

We use the T3-MSR score as one of the measures for evidencing attainment of a Tier 3 Gold PBIS Champion Model System. The first step toward developing a Tier 3 Gold PBIS Champion Model System is to assess the current state of your own system using the T3-MSR. You will use the results of this tool to perform a gap analysis and get an understanding of where your system is in relation to the five critical Tier 3 markers. It is important that you provide honest responses for all the T3-MSR items because the information gained from the rubric data is used to guide your next-step actions.

Who should complete the T3-MSR? To ensure accurate baseline information is collected, a PBIS Tier 3 sub-team should complete the rubric. If you do not have a PBIS Tier 3 sub-team established at the time of completing the baseline rubric, the administrator of the school should complete the initial rubric in collaboration with his or her school leadership team or other selected stakeholders.

TIER 3: THE FIVE PBIS TIER 3 MARKERS

This section presents each of the five Tier 3 PBIS markers, including the following details:

- Description of the marker
- Questions to consider in relation to the marker
- Assessing our current state: Where are we in relation to this marker?
- List of actions to advance the marker from current state to desired future and a reflection about next-step, high-leverage moves
- Cautions or red flags indicating that one or more areas of the marker may need to be addressed
- Examples from the field: challenges, practical solutions, and tools/resources used

LET'S GET STARTED WITH TIER 3 MARKERS

MARKER 1
Establish and Operate an Effective PBIS Tier 3 Sub-Team

Assemble a PBIS Tier 3 sub-team, composed of four members of the PBIS school-wide team (e.g., representation from administration, general education, special education, and a behavior specialist) who can commit to meeting for forty-five minutes to an hour once a week to plan, implement, and monitor general education and special education students receiving a Tier 3 intervention in the school. An administrator is an active member of this team and guarantees that the team members have the time to meet and the resources needed to be successful. The PBIS Tier 3 sub-team has a designated lead who helps organize the meetings and ensure that they are taking place using updated data in an organized and consistent fashion and that the information is being shared with all stakeholders. The Tier 3 sub-team can be composed of the same members as the Tier 2 sub-team.

Note

Some schools incorporate their academic and behavior tiered system team meetings together; that is sufficient as long as the Tier 3 behavior system component of the agenda is given the attention needed for successful Tier 3 intervention implementation.

Questions to Consider

Does our school have a PBIS Tier 3 sub-team? If yes, is our team operating effectively?

_____

_____

_____

Does the membership of our PBIS Tier 3 sub-team include an administrator, a staff member with expertise in creating behavior interventions, and representation from both general education and special education?

_____

_____

_____

Do our PBIS Tier 3 sub-team members understand the purpose of their role?

_____

_____

_____

Does our administrator actively support the PBIS Tier 3 sub-team by attending all meetings as well as supporting the decisions and work of the PBIS Tier 3 sub-team?

_____

_____

_____

Does our PBIS Tier 3 sub-team meet at least weekly for forty-five minutes to an hour and utilize a process to identify, progress monitor, and refine Tier 3 interventions based on the data?

_____

_____

_____

Assessing Our Current State:
Where Are We in Relation to Marker 1?

Marker 1: Establish and Operate Effective PBIS Tier 3 Sub-Team

Criteria	2 points	1 point	0 points	Score
PBIS Tier 3 sub-team is assembled.	The PBIS Tier 3 sub-team is composed of at least four members of the school-wide PBIS team. The Tier 3 sub-team includes representation from administration, general education, special education, and a behavior specialist who has expertise in identifying function of behavior and developing behavior interventions. The Tier 3 sub-team meets for forty-five minutes to an hour at least once a week to plan and monitor Tier 3 intervention implementation and effectiveness.	The PBIS Tier 3 sub-team is established, but meetings are held inconsistently and are not a priority. There is no representation from special education.	A PBIS Tier 3 sub-team does not exist at the school.	_____/2
Administrator support is evident.	An administrator is an active member of the PBIS Tier 3 sub-team, guaranteeing that the Tier 3 sub-team members have time to meet and the resources they need.	An administrator is a part of the Tier 3 sub-team but gets pulled away frequently from the meetings.	There is no administrator representation on the Tier 3 sub-team. An administrator does not attend Tier 3 sub-team meetings.	_____/2
A PBIS Tier 3 sub-team lead has been established.	The PBIS Tier 3 sub-team has a designated lead. The lead helps organize and ensure the Tier 3 sub-team meetings are taking	The Tier 3 sub-team has not yet designated a lead but an administrator	There is no Tier 3 sub-team lead established.	

Criteria	2 points	1 point	0 points	Score
	place and ensures a process utilizing data with a clear focus at every meeting. The lead helps ensure Tier 3 intervention information is being shared at least weekly with all stakeholders. The lead follows up on the commitments the Tier 3 sub-team members make during their weekly Tier 3 sub-team meetings.	helps facilitate the meetings at this time. There is no process in place to guide the meeting and keep the team on focus. Information from the meetings is not formally documented or shared with stakeholders.	Meetings are disorganized.	_____/2
				Total _____/6

**ACTIONS TO ESTABLISH AND OPERATE
AN EFFECTIVE PBIS TIER 3 SUB-TEAM**

- The members of the Tier 3 sub-team develop a common understanding of the definition of a Tier 3 intervention.
- The administrator shares the research, purpose, and goals of implementing Tier 3 interventions at the school.
- The members of the Tier 3 sub-team develop a focus (e.g., one of the focus items at every meeting is on monitoring each student receiving a Tier 3 intervention and adjusting the intervention as needed as a sub-team).
- The administrator and the members of the Tier 3 sub-team can articulate components necessary to establish an effective Tier 3 behavior system.
- The role and purpose of the PBIS Tier 3 sub-team is defined and articulated to the entire school staff.

(Continued)

(Continued)

- The PBIS Tier 3 sub-team includes *at least* three diverse staff members (e.g., representation from special education, general education, and support services) who are positive, influential, and committed to implementing Tier 3 interventions and supports.
- An administrator serves as an active member of the sub-team.
- At least one member of the PBIS Tier 3 sub-team has expertise in behavior intervention development and identifying function of behavior.
- The PBIS Tier 3 sub-team schedules meetings of forty-five minutes to an hour during the duty day or at an agreed-upon time, and the PBIS Tier 3 sub-team members adhere to the meeting schedule.
- The PBIS Tier 3 sub-team members commit to establishing and following a selected agenda/checklist/process and norms for each meeting.
- An administrator allows time for the PBIS Tier 3 sub-team lead to organize and prepare for PBIS Tier 3 sub-team meetings. The lead will help facilitate the meetings, monitor the work of the sub-team by ensuring weekly meetings are held, and follow up on commitments made by the PBIS Tier 3 sub-team.
- The PBIS Tier 3 sub-team shares updates (five to ten minutes) with the staff during every staff or department meeting.
- PBIS Tier 3 sub-team membership is offered as an adjunct duty or replacement for supervision duty.
- A stipend is provided to the Tier 3 sub-team lead.
- An additional preparation period is provided at the secondary level.
- Stakeholders are invited to provide input to the Tier 3 sub-team meetings.

CAUTION

If you find one or more of the following conditions or situations occurring at your school, view the condition/situation as a red flag signaling that one or more areas of this marker—Establish and Operate an Effective PBIS Tier 3 Sub-Team—may need to be addressed.

RED FLAGS

- The PBIS Tier 3 sub-team has been established but meets for compliance reasons only; the team members do not believe the Tier 3 behavior system will work for students needing that level of intervention.
- The PBIS Tier 3 sub-team was thrown together and does not meet regularly to review Tier 3 behavior data.

- Meetings are not focused on outcomes.
- The administrator and PBIS Tier 3 sub-team members are unclear as to what it takes to implement an effective Tier 3 behavior system.
- The PBIS Tier 3 sub-team does not include a member with behavior expertise.
- The administrator never or rarely attends PBIS Tier 3 sub-team meetings.
- The administrator is not supportive, as evidenced by his or her behaviors and actions; and quality of the decisions and work of the PBIS Tier 3 sub-team is low.
- Decisions are based on emotion, rather than evidence.
- No evidence exists of an agenda, checklists, processes, norms, and/or actions taken for each team meeting.
- PBIS Tier 3 sub-team meetings are canceled due to other meetings taking priority.
- PBIS Tier 3 sub-team meetings are scheduled during non-duty times, and/or PBIS Tier 2 sub-team members are assigned supervision duty or other responsibilities that conflict with PBIS Tier 3 sub-team meeting times and no coverage is provided.
- PBIS Tier 3 sub-team meetings are not focused, and messaging to the entire staff about the work is not clear. *(The consequence is that team members begin to drop out of being part of the team because the messaging to school staff is not clear—thus reflecting on them in a negative light.)*
- The administrator and PBIS Tier 3 sub-team cannot articulate the purpose for Tier 3 interventions and the relationship to student success.
- The PBIS Tier 3 sub-team does not provide updates to stakeholders on a regular basis, resulting in loss of buy-in.
- The PBIS Tier 3 sub-team has not adequately identified all the students receiving a Tier 3 intervention at the school.
- The discussions are focused on one student only instead of on the progress of all students receiving a Tier 3 intervention.
- Data are not updated for the meetings.

Based on our assessment of the current state for this marker and the suggested list of actions and red flags, what should our next move be?

_____

_____

_____

(Continued)

(Continued)

_____

_____

_____

_____

_____

_____

_____

_____

FROM THE FIELD: MARKER 1—ESTABLISH AND OPERATE AN EFFECTIVE PBIS TIER 3 SUB-TEAM

Challenge: The PBIS Tier 3 sub-team did not have a consistent understanding of how to conduct productive PBIS Tier 3 sub-team meetings. Team members already felt overwhelmed with the work they had to do with Tier 2 intervention monitoring. In this case, the PBIS Tier 3 sub-team was an expansion of the PBIS Tier 2 sub-team. The PBIS Tier 3 sub-team had a designated lead and good representation of staff in attendance to the meetings but felt overwhelmed by the data and focus of each meeting. The way the meetings were currently running seemed like a waste of their time.

How would you address this challenge?

_____

_____

_____

_____

_____

_____

_____

_____

_____

_____

꒰ఞ꒱

Practical solution: The administrator decided to make the role of the PBIS Tier 3 sub-team lead an adjunct duty. The administrator provided coverage and/or compensation for the lead to prepare for the weekly sub-team meetings. In addition, the PBIS Tier 3 sub-team developed a structure to review each student receiving a Tier 2 intervention.

Tool/resource used: PBIS Tier 2 and Tier 3 Behavior Data Wall

What is it? The PBIS Tier 2 and Tier 3 Behavior Data Wall is a visual tool to assist the PBIS Tier 3 sub-team members with covering the components for each student on a Tier 3 intervention during their PBIS Tier 3 sub-team meetings. It is a helpful resource to ensure the Tier 3 sub-team stays on focus and logs next-step actions and timelines for each student.

PBIS Tier 2 and Tier 3 Behavior Data Wall

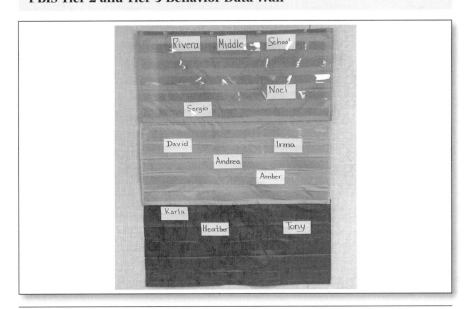

Source: Courtesy of Rivera Middle School PBIS Team

Note: Detailed instructions on how to utilize this process are provided on the next page.

PBIS Tier 2 and Tier 3 Data Wall Instructions

Follow these steps for each Tier 2 and 3 sub-team meeting:

Step 1: Utilize a colored pocket chart; each color on the chart represents a PBIS tiered system intervention intensity level of the school (green—Tier 1, yellow—Tier 2, and red—Tier 3).

Step 2: Identify all students receiving a Tier 2 and Tier 3 intervention at your school and put their names on individual note cards (i.e., each student has his or her own card).

Step 3: For students receiving Tier 2 interventions, place their name card in a yellow pocket; for students receiving Tier 3 interventions, place their name card in a red pocket. (Student name cards can be moved to the Tier 1 area of the chart when their intervention data consistently show they have responded to the Tier 2 or Tier 3 intervention and are responding at the Tier 1 level.) *Please make sure this pocket chart is posted in a confidential setting.*

Step 4: The PBIS sub-team lead facilitates the process for each student based on the updated data.

Step 5: The focus of the sub-team is on deciding if the students will remain on the level of intervention they are receiving, move to another level, exit from the intervention, or receive other supports. The sub-team lead will move the cards accordingly based on the discussion (e.g., a student on a Tier 3 special education behavior support plan [red pocket] who is responding to the Tier 3 intervention and not getting into any trouble can be moved to the green section of the pocket chart for that week based on the data. The sub-team can go further and put a green dot sticker on a student's card in the red pocket to indicate the student is responding to the behavior support plan). *Note: Placing a student's card in the green section of this pocket chart does not mean taking the student off the behavior support plan he or she is responding to. It means the student is responding that week without getting into trouble. Now, if the student is in green for months, that may be an indicator that the Individualized Education Program (IEP) team needs to meet to discuss if a behavior goal on the IEP instead of a behavior support plan would suffice for that particular example. However, this is a case-by-case discussion for each student.*

Step 6: Log the progress of the students using Excel, Google Sheets, or another progress monitoring tool of your choice as you are going through this process, and make sure the record is available for all stakeholders involved with the Tier 3 intervention for referencing and providing input purposes.

MARKER 2
Establish a Culture and
Expectation for Supporting All Students

The PBIS Tier 3 sub-team will establish a culture where staff feel safe to ask for support for students needing Tier 3 interventions. Staff will understand the complexity of students needing Tier 3 interventions and understand their role in supporting them instead of feeling ineffective as teachers if they need help. The expectation on campus from the leadership is clear and will reflect supporting all students, not just the ones who behave. Feedback and input are gathered from staff on a regular basis to gauge the pulse of the culture.

೩ೲ

Questions to Consider

Are our staff aware of the expectation from school leadership for supporting all students with behavior needs at the school?

_____

_____

_____

Do our staff understand the meaning of Tier 3 interventions and their role in implementation?

_____

_____

_____

Do our staff feel safe to ask for support when they need help with a student needing Tier 3 supports?

_____

_____

_____

(Continued)

(Continued)

Are our staff given ongoing opportunities to provide feedback, offer suggestions, and make decisions regarding Tier 3 intervention implementation?

_____

_____

_____

Is there opportunity for our staff to gauge the pulse of the school culture when severe behaviors of a handful of students are impacting the school culture?

_____

_____

_____

Assessing Our Current State: Where Are We in Relation to Marker 2?

Marker 2: Establish a Culture and Expectation for Supporting All Students

Criteria	2 points	1 point	0 points	Score
A Culture Supporting All Students	At least 80 percent of the school staff understand, support, and have buy-in for Tier 3 implementation. Staff feel safe asking for support for students needing a Tier 3 intervention.	At least 50 percent of the school staff understand and support Tier 3 implementation.	The majority of the staff do not understand or support Tier 3 implementation.	_____/2
Staff Expectation	The expectation by the administration that all students (general education and special education) receiving Tier 3 interventions will be supported at the school is clear and consistent.	The expectation by the administration about Tier 3 implementation is inconsistent.	The leadership has not made the expectation clear.	_____/2

Criteria	2 points	1 point	0 points	Score
Staff Input	Staff input on Tier 3 implementation is gathered and considered by the Tier 3 sub-team. Staff members are provided opportunity to provide honest feedback on the impact Tier 3 implementation may be having on them.	Staff input is gathered inconsistently or not considered.	Staff input is not gathered.	____/2
				Total ____/6

ACTIONS TO ESTABLISH A CULTURE AND EXPECTATION FOR SUPPORTING ALL STUDENTS

- Recognize the need for PBIS Tier 3 implementation at your school
- Clarify your administration's expectation for how students needing Tier 3 interventions will receive the support they need to access their education
- Provide staff with an overview of the research that supports Tier 3 implementation
- Provide ongoing training that supports Tier 3 implementation
- Designate a portion of each staff or department meeting agenda for teachers to receive updates on Tier 3 implementation and effectiveness
- Clarify misconceptions about Tier 3 implementation
- Create ongoing opportunities for faculty to provide feedback, offer suggestions, and make decisions regarding PBIS Tier 3 processes
- Create a method for staff to provide ongoing honest input to the PBIS Tier 3 sub-team regarding Tier 3 intervention implementation
- Share Tier 3 intervention behavior data with staff and stakeholders at least monthly
- Clearly communicate and message all PBIS Tier 3 information in a timely fashion
- Educate staff on the procedures and protocols for referring students for Tier 3 interventions

(Continued)

(Continued)

- Ensure the role of the teacher in the Tier 3 intervention is clear, practical, and consistent
- Give staff opportunity to provide safe input on the impact of Tier 3 implementation on the school culture

CAUTION

If you find one or more of the following conditions or situations occurring at your school, view the condition/situation as a red flag signaling that one or more areas of this marker—Establish a Culture and Expectation for Supporting All Students—may need to be addressed.

RED FLAGS

- Staff are directed to help implement Tier 3 interventions but do not know what it entails.
- Tier 3 sub-team members serve for compliance reasons only and do not believe that Tier 3 implementation will help improve their school's system or that it is useful as an improvement strategy.
- Staff do not understand their role in the Tier 3 implementation.
- Misconceptions about Tier 3 implementation are not addressed.
- Administrators are not clear on their expectation for implementation of Tier 3 interventions.
- Staff do not understand the differences between special education and general education interventions.
- Staff are beginning to feel as if one or two students are running the school and nothing is being done about it.
- Staff are feeling as if they are being blamed for students not responding to Tier 3 interventions.
- Staff feel afraid to share that they need support because they feel that it is a reflection of their effectiveness.
- Teachers are beginning to feel as if getting the union involved is the only way they will receive support.

✥✥

Based on our assessment of the current state for this marker and the suggested list of actions and red flags, what should our next move be?

_____

_____

_____

_____

_____

_____

_____

_____

_____

_____

✥✥

FROM THE FIELD: MARKER 2—ESTABLISH A CULTURE AND EXPECTATION FOR SUPPORTING ALL STUDENTS

Challenge: A student at the school was demonstrating the need for an intensive individualized intervention. This student's behavior had escalated to the point where the teachers felt as if he was running the school and the administration was doing nothing about it. It was beginning to impact the school culture. All the staff knew who this student was but did not understand why he was behaving this way and why he was still attending the school.

✥✥

How would you address this challenge?

_____

_____

(Continued)

(Continued)

_____

_____

_____

_____

_____

_____

_____

_____

&&

Practical solution: The PBIS Tier 3 sub-team wanted to address this situation in a timely fashion so that the misconceptions from the staff did not negatively impact the school culture. They developed an anonymous staff survey to collect honest feedback from the staff so that they could address the misconceptions or the areas of need based on the majority input from the staff. They also used this information to develop professional learning opportunities for the staff on Tier 3 intervention implementation at the school.

Tool/resource used: Tier 3 Implementation Survey: Staff Version

What is it? The Tier 3 Implementation Survey: Staff Version is a short survey that is given to staff anonymously throughout the school year by the PBIS Tier 3 sub-team to gauge the pulse of the staff culture in relation to Tier 3 implementation at the school and create actions in response to the gathered feedback.

Tier 3 Implementation Survey: Staff Version		
Survey Items	**Agree (A), Neutral (N), Disagree (D)**	**Reason for your rating:**
1. I understand why we provide Tier 3 interventions to students demonstrating intensive behaviors at school.		
2. I feel safe asking for support if I am working with a student who needs a Tier 3 intervention.		
3. I have a colleague having a challenging time with a student needing a Tier 3 intervention.		
4. Administration is supporting the staff with students who need a Tier 3 intervention.		
5. I feel like students who need Tier 3 interventions at our school are out of control.		
6. I understand the special education processes and laws behind implementing Tier 3 interventions for special education students.		
7. I feel equipped and understand my role in helping students needing Tier 3 interventions.		
8. I understand the process for asking for help with a student needing Tier 3 interventions at our school.		
9. I believe that all students deserve the behavioral supports they need to access their education.		
10. I feel like our staff need more professional development on the implementation of Tier 3 interventions at our school.		

Marker 3
Conduct a Tier 3 Resource Inventory

The PBIS Tier 3 sub-team conducts a Tier 3 resource inventory utilizing data and input from stakeholders on a regular basis. The purpose of this inventory is to have a formal method of assessing and allocating Tier 3 resources at your school for general education and special education. There is a process in place to adjust the resources based on the Tier 3 intervention needs of the students.

Questions to Consider

Has our PBIS Tier 3 sub-team conducted a Tier 3 resource inventory?

_____

_____

_____

Does a formal method exist for assessing and allocating our school's Tier 3 resources?

_____

_____

_____

Does the allocation of resources adjust based on the individualized needs of students receiving general education?

_____

_____

_____

Does the allocation of resources adjust based on the individualized needs of students receiving special education?

_____

_____

_____

Assessing Our Current State:
Where Are We in Relation to Marker 3?

Marker 3: Conduct a Tier 3 Resource Inventory

Criteria	2 points	1 point	0 points	Score
Tier 3 Resource Inventory Procedure	The PBIS Tier 3 sub-team has an established procedure for conducting a Tier 3 resource inventory on a regular basis. Data and stakeholder input are utilized to assess and allocate Tier 3 resources.	The PBIS Tier 3 sub-team has an inconsistent procedure in place for conducting a Tier 3 resource inventory. Data and stakeholder input are not utilized for this procedure.	The PBIS Tier 3 sub-team does not have a procedure in place for conducting a Tier 3 resource inventory.	_____/2
General Education and Special Education	The PBIS Tier 3 sub-team considers both general education and special education resources as it is assessing and allocating Tier 3 resources. The PBIS Tier 3 sub-team understands the differences between general education and special education resources.	The PBIS Tier 3 sub-team inconsistently considers both general education and special education resources as it is assessing and allocating Tier 3 resources. The PBIS Tier 3 sub-team does not understand the differences between general education and special education resources.	General education and special education resources are not understood or considered during the allotment of Tier 3 resources.	_____/2
Process to Adjust Tier 3 Resources	The PBIS Tier 3 sub-team has a process in place to adjust Tier 3 resources based on student individualized behavior needs.	The PBIS Tier 3 sub-team meets at least bi-monthly but does not use data to make decisions about placing or exiting students from Tier 3 interventions.	The PBIS Tier 3 sub-team does not have a process in place to adjust Tier 3 resources at the school.	_____/2
				Total _____/6

**ACTIONS TO CONDUCT A TIER 3
RESOURCE INVENTORY**

- Make sure your Tier 3 sub-team meets on a regular basis
- Make sure there is representation from both general education and special education as you are conducting a Tier 3 resource inventory
- Make sure you know all students receiving Tier 3 interventions at the school before conducting a Tier 3 resource inventory
- Update all information needed before meeting
- Make sure the administration is part of these meetings
- Have a process in place to adjust how resources are being utilized based on the data and stakeholder input

---

CAUTION

If you find one or more of the following conditions or situations occurring at your school, view the condition/situation as a red flag signaling that one or more areas of this marker—Conduct a Tier 3 Resource Inventory— may need to be addressed.

RED FLAGS

- Only meeting at the beginning of the school year
- Not having all information to allot resources
- Allocating resources as you have always done without considering general education and special education student individualized needs
- Not having administration present
- Not having representation of both general education and special education

---

Based on our assessment of the current state for this marker and the suggested list of actions and red flags, what should our next move be?

_____

_____

_____

_____

_____

_____

_____

_____

_____

_____

_____

FROM THE FIELD: MARKER 3— CONDUCT A TIER 3 RESOURCE INVENTORY

Challenge: The PBIS Tier 3 sub-team did not have an organized procedure in place to assess and allot the Tier 3 resources available for students at the school for both general education and special education. As a result, emotional decisions were made about available resources rather than data and stakeholder input being considered based on the needs of the students.

How would you address this challenge?

_____

_____

_____

_____

_____

_____

_____

(Continued)

(Continued)

_____

_____

_____

—————————————— ❧❦❧ ——————————————

Practical solution: The PBIS Tier 3 sub-team developed the Tier 3 Resource Inventory Check Form to utilize on at least a monthly basis to make sure the resources at the school were allotted to the students in both general education and special education needing individualized interventions.

Tool/resource used: Tier 3 Resource Inventory Check Form

What is it? The Tier 3 Resource Inventory Check Form is used at least once a month by the PBIS Tier 3 sub-team and other stakeholders representing both general education and special education in order to have a guide or frame to follow as discussions and decisions are made about Tier 3 intervention resource allotment at the school based on student need.

Date of Tier 3 Resource Inventory Check: _____
\# of students currently receiving a general education Tier 3 intervention: _____
\# of students currently receiving a special education Tier 3 intervention: _____

Tier 3 Resource Inventory Check

Resources	General Education	Special Education	Additional Notes
Time			
Money			
Materials			
People			
Rooms			
Resources			
Curriculum			
Expertise			
Other			

Note: Complete based on needed resources.

Marker 4
Establish a Tier 3 Timely Response Plan

The PBIS Tier 3 sub-team will establish a timely response plan for a student whose behaviors are escalating. The PBIS Tier 3 sub-team members work with the stakeholders to develop a plan for the student. The staff understand that within twenty-four hours of requesting support from the Tier 3 sub-team, the team will meet and begin the development of a timely response plan with the goal of putting it in place by the following day or as soon as possible within the week the plan is initiated. The Tier 3 sub-team will monitor frequently and adjust the new plan accordingly based on implementation. The administration is an active member of this plan and ensures the Tier 3 sub-team members have the resources they need in order to develop and implement a plan in a timely fashion.

Questions to Consider

Does our school have a Tier 3 sub-team established that meets in a timely fashion to plan a response for a student demonstrating Tier 3 intervention needs?

_____

_____

_____

Does our school have a time frame as a guide for responding to intensive student behavior intervention needs?

_____

_____

_____

Does our school have an administration that actively supports and provides the resources necessary to ensure the plan is established and implemented in a timely fashion?

_____

_____

_____

Assessing Our Current State:
Where Are We in Relation to Marker 4?

Marker 4: Establish a Tier 3 Timely Response Plan

Criteria	2 points	1 point	0 points	Score
Timely Response Plan	The PBIS Tier 3 sub-team establishes a timely response plan for a student whose behaviors are escalating. The PBIS Tier 3 sub-team works with the stakeholders to develop a plan for students.	The PBIS Tier 3 sub-team establishes a response plan for a student whose behaviors are escalating, but the team members do not consider all stakeholder input and their response is not always timely.	The PBIS Tier 3 sub-team does not establish a timely response plan for a student whose behaviors are escalating.	_____/2
Timeline for Response and Monitoring	The PBIS Tier 3 sub-team meets and begins development of a timely response plan within twenty-four hours of receiving a request for support from a staff member or other stakeholder. The PBIS Tier 3 sub-team puts the response plan in place by the following day or as soon as possible within the week the plan is initiated. The PBIS Tier 3 sub-team monitors the plan frequently and adjusts the plan accordingly based on implementation.	The PBIS Tier 3 sub-team has an inconsistent timeline and monitoring system in place for students needing a Tier 3 timely response plan.	There is no established timeline for response or monitoring in place.	_____/2
Administrator Support	The administration is an active member of this plan and ensures the Tier 3 sub-team members have the resources they need in order to develop and implement a plan in a timely fashion.	The administration is inconsistently involved with the development and implementation of a timely response plan.	The administration is not an active member of the Tier 3 sub-team, therefore making the efforts of the Tier 3 sub-team difficult to implement in a timely fashion.	_____/2
				Total _____/6

ACTIONS TO ESTABLISH A TIER 3 TIMELY RESPONSE PLAN

- Have administration support
- Make sure there is a system in place for staff or stakeholders to request support in intensive behavior cases
- Make sure there is representation of stakeholders needed to help plan for the student
- Make sure resources are allotted to help the student based on the developed plan
- Make sure the PBIS Tier 3 sub-team members hold themselves to the timelines
- Begin implementation to help the student within a week
- Establish a monitoring and adjustment plan
- Ensure ongoing communication

CAUTION

If you find one or more of the following conditions or situations occurring at your school, view the condition/situation as a red flag signaling that one or more areas of this marker—Establish a Tier 3 Timely Response Plan—may need to be addressed.

RED FLAGS

- Administration is not involved.
- Stakeholders do not meet until the behaviors escalate to an extremely challenging point.
- Resources are not made available.
- The PBIS Tier 3 sub-team members have excuses for why they cannot meet.
- Adequate stakeholders are not present at the meeting.
- The plan is established, but there is no follow-through.
- There is limited collaboration between general education and special education.
- Responding differently for parents/guardians who understand the laws and their child's rights.

Based on our assessment of the current state for this marker and the suggested list of actions and red flags, what should our next move be?

_____

_____

(Continued)

(Continued)

_____

_____

_____

_____

_____

_____

_____

_____

_____

ๆๆ

FROM THE FIELD: MARKER 4— ESTABLISH A TIER 3 TIMELY RESPONSE PLAN

Challenge: The staff was not clear of the role and referral process for the development of a timely response plan for a student demonstrating the need for a Tier 3 intervention.

ๆๆ

How would you address this challenge?

_____

_____

_____

_____

_____

_____

_____

_____

_____

_____

Practical solution: The PBIS Tier 3 sub-team developed a flowchart to help staff understand when it was appropriate for them to request support for a student demonstrating a need for a Tier 3 intervention. They also wanted to clarify the differences between responses for general education and special education students needing Tier 3 interventions in a timely fashion.

Tool/resource used: Tier 3 Response Plan Flowchart

What is it? The Tier 3 Response Plan Flowchart was developed to help staff understand how to ask for help for both general and special education students needing a timely response for intensive behaviors.

Tier 3 Response Plan Flowchart "3-day response rule"

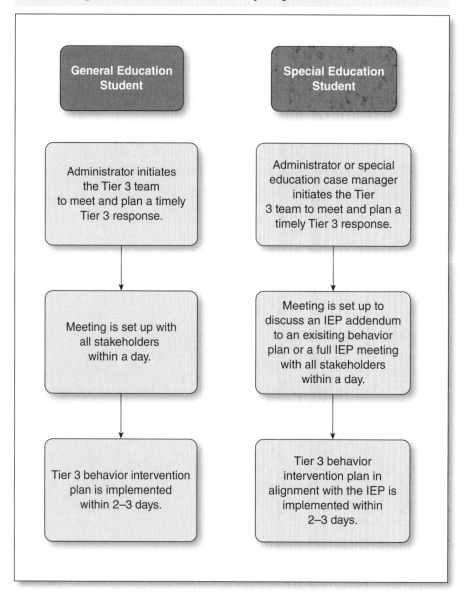

Marker 5
Establish a Tier 3 Fidelity Check Process

The PBIS Tier 3 sub-team establishes a Tier 3 fidelity check process to ensure Tier 3 interventions are being implemented with fidelity for students receiving both general education and special education services. Fidelity of implementation is evaluated at multiple levels (e.g., administration, stakeholder/staff, student, and parent/guardian). The PBIS Tier 3 sub-team helps ensure all stakeholders/staff are implementing their role in the Tier 3 intervention with fidelity by frequent check-ins, observations, and opportunities for the staff/stakeholders to provide input, make suggestions, and request additional supports.

❧

Questions to Consider

Does a method exist for our Tier 3 sub-team to monitor the fidelity of Tier 3 intervention implementation?

_____

_____

_____

Is Tier 3 intervention fidelity data reviewed by the Tier 3 sub-team at least on a weekly basis?

_____

_____

_____

Does a process exist to improve Tier 3 implementation fidelity based on the fidelity data collected and analyzed by the Tier 3 sub-team?

_____

_____

_____

Are our staff trained to better address Tier 3 implementation fidelity?

_____

_____

_____

❧

Assessing Our Current State:
Where Are We in Relation to Marker 5?

Marker 5: Establish a Tier 3 Fidelity Check Process

Criteria	2 points	1 point	0 points	Score
Fidelity Check Process	The PBIS Tier 3 sub-team has established a fidelity check process to ensure Tier 3 interventions are being implemented with fidelity. The fidelity check process includes the review for students receiving both general education and special education services.	The PBIS Tier 3 sub-team is in the process of developing a fidelity check process for Tier 3 interventions.	No fidelity check process exists for Tier 3 interventions.	_____/2
Multiple Levels	Fidelity of implementation is evaluated at multiple levels (e.g., administration, stakeholder/staff, student, and parent/guardian).	Fidelity of Tier 3 implementation is only evaluated by the administration at this time.	Fidelity of Tier 3 implementation is not evaluated at multiple levels.	_____/2
Staff Fidelity	About 80 percent of the staff comprising both general and special education staff have bought into implementing their role in Tier 3 interventions with fidelity. The PBIS Tier 3 sub-team helps ensure the staff/stakeholders are implementing the Tier 3 interventions with fidelity by frequent check-ins, observations, and creating ongoing opportunities to gather feedback and provide additional supports and trainings.	About 50 percent of the staff have bought into implementing their role in Tier 3 interventions with fidelity. There is no method in place to ensure Tier 3 interventions are being implemented with fidelity by staff in both general education and special education.	The majority of the staff do not believe in the implementation of Tier 3 interventions.	_____/2
				Total _____/6

ACTIONS TO ESTABLISH A TIER 3
FIDELITY CHECK PROCESS

- Develop a process to monitor Tier 3 intervention implementation at least weekly (e.g., Tier 3 Intervention Fidelity Check Log)
- Include monitoring fidelity of Tier 3 interventions as an agenda item during Tier 3 sub-team meetings
- Include monitoring fidelity of Tier 3 interventions in both general education and special education
- Educate staff on the fidelity of Tier 3 intervention implementation and provide ongoing training and support as needed throughout the year on a case-by-case basis
- Send reminders to staff about implementing Tier 3 interventions with fidelity
- Have one-on-one meetings with staff who need additional support in regard to the implementation of Tier 3 interventions
- Gain administrator assistance working with resistant staff members
- Establish buy-in during staff meetings (e.g., educate staff on the importance of implementing Tier 3 interventions with fidelity)
- Ensure Tier 3 intervention implementation is clear, consistent, and practical for staff
- Provide staff feedback on implementation and help follow up with other stakeholders (e.g., parent/guardian)

CAUTION

If you find one or more of the following conditions or situations occurring at your school, view the condition/situation as a red flag signaling that one or more areas of this marker—Establish a Tier 3 Fidelity Check Process—may need to be addressed.

RED FLAGS

- Staff do not believe in implementing Tier 3 interventions.
- Staff do not understand the similarities and differences between general education and special education Tier 3 interventions.
- Staff do not follow through with the Tier 3 intervention implementation.
- Communication on student progress is nonexistent.
- Students do not understand their role in the Tier 3 intervention.

(Continued)

(Continued)

- Progress of SMART (Strategic and Specific, Measurable, Attainable/ Achievable, Results-Oriented and Relevant, and Time-Bound) goals is not reviewed with the students or communicated to the stakeholders.
- Tier 3 interventions are not delivered consistently.
- No positive outcomes have come about as a result of Tier 3 interventions not being implemented with fidelity.
- Incentives for Tier 3 interventions are not provided consistently for students meeting their SMART goals.
- No procedures exist to continue a Tier 3 intervention when a staff member is absent.
- Tier 3 intervention is presented as a "gotcha" instead of a practice that provides additional support.

—————— ❧❧ ——————

Based on our assessment of the current state for this marker and the suggested list of actions and red flags, what should our next move be?

_____

_____

_____

_____

_____

_____

_____

_____

_____

—————— ❧❧ ——————

FROM THE FIELD: MARKER 5— ESTABLISH A TIER 3 FIDELITY CHECK PROCESS

Challenge: The PBIS Tier 3 sub-team did not have a method to ensure the Tier 3 interventions were being implemented with fidelity. No method existed to check in with staff/stakeholders to review the adult role in whether or not the Tier 3 intervention was effective.

How would you address this challenge?

_____

_____

_____

_____

_____

_____

_____

_____

_____

_____

Practical solution: The Tier 3 sub-team developed the Tier 3 Intervention Fidelity Check Log, which was completed by the Tier 3 sub-team lead based on the input from the stakeholders from both general education and special education receiving Tier 3 interventions. The Tier 3 sub-team lead provides a hard copy, emails, or shares a document online with the staff/stakeholders involved in the Tier 3 implementation every Friday. Gathering this Tier 3 implementation fidelity data helped the Tier 3 sub-team address any areas that needed improvement for the Tier 3 intervention to be effective. It also allowed them to decide what types of professional development or coaching opportunities needed to take place to improve the fidelity of the Tier 3 interventions offered.

Tool/resource used: Tier 3 Intervention Fidelity Check Log

What is it? The Tier 3 Intervention Fidelity Check Log is designed to monitor the fidelity of Tier 3 intervention implementation and identify areas within the Tier 3 intervention that need refining for both general education and special education Tier 3 interventions. The PBIS Tier 3 sub-team reviews this information at least weekly and makes modifications or suggestions to improve Tier 3 implementation based on the collected fidelity feedback.

Note

Each letter in the Tier 3 Intervention Fidelity Check Log represents a stakeholder that has a role in implementation for each identified Tier 3 intervention. Circle if the stakeholder implemented her or his role with fidelity or leave blank for unsuccessful implementation.

Tier 3 Intervention Fidelity Check Log: Month _____

S = Student   T = Teacher   P = Parent   A = Administrator   O = Other

Special Education Student Tier 3 Intervention List	Week of _____	Week of _____	Week of _____	Week of _____	Week of _____
Student Name:	*How did we do?* Monday S T P A O Tuesday S T P A O Wednesday S T P A O Thursday S T P A O Friday S T P A O	*How did we do?* Monday S T P A O Tuesday S T P A O Wednesday S T P A O Thursday S T P A O Friday S T P A O	*How did we do?* Monday S T P A O Tuesday S T P A O Wednesday S T P A O Thursday S T P A O Friday S T P A O	*How did we do?* Monday S T P A O Tuesday S T P A O Wednesday S T P A O Thursday S T P A O Friday S T P A O	*How did we do?* Monday S T P A O Tuesday S T P A O Wednesday S T P A O Thursday S T P A O Friday S T P A O
Student Name:	*How did we do?* Monday S T P A O Tuesday S T P A O Wednesday S T P A O Thursday S T P A O Friday S T P A O	*How did we do?* Monday S T P A O Tuesday S T P A O Wednesday S T P A O Thursday S T P A O Friday S T P A O	*How did we do?* Monday S T P A O Tuesday S T P A O Wednesday S T P A O Thursday S T P A O Friday S T P A O	*How did we do?* Monday S T P A O Tuesday S T P A O Wednesday S T P A O Thursday S T P A O Friday S T P A O	*How did we do?* Monday S T P A O Tuesday S T P A O Wednesday S T P A O Thursday S T P A O Friday S T P A O

Tier 3 Intervention Fidelity Check Log: Month _____				
S = Student T = Teacher P = Parent A = Administrator O = Other				
General Education Student *Tier 3 Intervention List*	Week of _____	Week of _____	Week of _____	Week of _____	Week of _____
Student Name:	*How did we do?* Monday S T P A O Tuesday S T P A O Wednesday S T P A O Thursday S T P A O Friday S T P A O	*How did we do?* Monday S T P A O Tuesday S T P A O Wednesday S T P A O Thursday S T P A O Friday S T P A O	*How did we do?* Monday S T P A O Tuesday S T P A O Wednesday S T P A O Thursday S T P A O Friday S T P A O	*How did we do?* Monday S T P A O Tuesday S T P A O Wednesday S T P A O Thursday S T P A O Friday S T P A O	*How did we do?* Monday S T P A O Tuesday S T P A O Wednesday S T P A O Thursday S T P A O Friday S T P A O
Student Name:	*How did we do?* Monday S T P A O Tuesday S T P A O Wednesday S T P A O Thursday S T P A O Friday S T P A O	*How did we do?* Monday S T P A O Tuesday S T P A O Wednesday S T P A O Thursday S T P A O Friday S T P A O	*How did we do?* Monday S T P A O Tuesday S T P A O Wednesday S T P A O Thursday S T P A O Friday S T P A O	*How did we do?* Monday S T P A O Tuesday S T P A O Wednesday S T P A O Thursday S T P A O Friday S T P A O	*How did we do?* Monday S T P A O Tuesday S T P A O Wednesday S T P A O Thursday S T P A O Friday S T P A O

TIER 3 MARKERS SCORING RUBRIC (T3-MSR) FULL VERSION

Criteria	2 points	1 point	0 points	Score
Marker 1: Establish and Operate Effective PBIS Tier 3 Sub-Team				
PBIS Tier 3 sub-team is assembled.	The PBIS Tier 3 sub-team is composed of at least four members of the school-wide PBIS team. The Tier 3 sub-team includes representation from administration, general education, special education, and a behavior specialist who has expertise in identifying function of behavior and developing behavior interventions. The Tier 3 sub-team meets for forty-five minutes to an hour at least once a week to plan and monitor Tier 3 intervention implementation and effectiveness.	The PBIS Tier 3 sub-team is established, but meetings are held inconsistently and are not a priority. There is no representation from special education.	A PBIS Tier 3 sub-team does not exist at the school.	_____/2
Administrator support is evident.	An administrator is an active member of the PBIS Tier 3 sub-team, guaranteeing that the Tier 3 sub-team members have time to meet and the resources they need.	An administrator is a part of the Tier 3 sub-team but gets pulled away frequently from the meetings.	There is no administrator representation on the Tier 3 sub-team. An administrator does not attend Tier 3 sub-team meetings.	_____/2
A PBIS Tier 3 sub-team lead has been established.	The PBIS Tier 3 sub-team has a designated lead. The lead helps organize and ensure the Tier 3 sub-team meetings are taking place and ensures a process utilizing data with a clear focus at every meeting.	The Tier 3 sub-team has not yet designated a lead but an administrator helps facilitate the meetings at this time.	There is no Tier 3 sub-team lead established.	

Criteria	2 points	1 point	0 points	Score
	The lead helps ensure Tier 3 intervention information is being shared at least weekly with all stakeholders. The lead follows up on the commitments the Tier 3 sub-team members make during their weekly Tier 3 sub-team meetings.	There is no process in place to guide the meeting and keep the team on focus. Information from the meetings is not formally documented or shared with stakeholders.	Meetings are disorganized.	____/2
				Total ____/6
Marker 2: Establish a Culture and Expectation for Supporting All Students				
A Culture Supporting All Students	At least 80 percent of the school staff understand, support, and have buy-in for Tier 3 implementation. Staff feel safe asking for support for students needing a Tier 3 intervention.	At least 50 percent of the school staff understand and support Tier 3 implementation.	The majority of the staff do not understand or support Tier 3 implementation.	____/2
Staff Expectation	The expectation by the administration that all students (general education and special education) receiving Tier 3 interventions will be supported at the school is clear and consistent.	The expectation by the administration about Tier 3 implementation is inconsistent.	The leadership has not made the expectation clear.	____/2
Staff Input	Staff input on Tier 3 implementation is gathered and considered by the Tier 3 sub-team. Staff members are provided opportunity to provide honest feedback on the impact Tier 3 implementation may be having on them.	Staff input is gathered inconsistently or not considered.	Staff input is not gathered.	____/2
				Total ____/6

(Continued)

(Continued)

Criteria	2 points	1 point	0 points	Score
Marker 3: Conduct a Tier 3 Resource Inventory				
Tier 3 Resource Inventory Procedure	The PBIS Tier 3 sub-team has an established procedure for conducting a Tier 3 resource inventory on a regular basis. Data and stakeholder input are utilized to assess and allocate Tier 3 resources.	The PBIS Tier 3 sub-team has an inconsistent procedure in place for conducting a Tier 3 resource inventory. Data and stakeholder input are not utilized for this procedure.	The PBIS Tier 3 sub-team does not have a procedure in place for conducting a Tier 3 resource inventory.	_____/2
General Education and Special Education	The PBIS Tier 3 sub-team considers both general education and special education resources as it is assessing and allocating Tier 3 resources. The PBIS Tier 3 sub-team understands the differences between general education and special education resources.	The PBIS Tier 3 sub-team inconsistently considers both general education and special education resources as it is assessing and allocating Tier 3 resources. The PBIS Tier 3 sub-team does not understand the differences between general education and special education resources.	General education and special education resources are not understood or considered during the allotment of Tier 3 resources.	_____/2
Process to Adjust Tier 3 Resources	The PBIS Tier 3 sub-team has a process in place to adjust Tier 3 resources based on student individualized behavior needs.	The PBIS Tier 3 sub-team meets at least bi-monthly but does not use data to make decisions about placing or exiting students from Tier 3 interventions.	The PBIS Tier 3 sub-team does not have a process in place to adjust Tier 3 resources at the school.	_____/2
				Total _____/6

Criteria	2 points	1 point	0 points	Score
Marker 4: Establish a Tier 3 Timely Response Plan				
Timely Response Plan	The PBIS Tier 3 sub-team establishes a timely response plan for a student whose behaviors are escalating. The PBIS Tier 3 sub-team works with the stakeholders to develop a plan for students.	The PBIS Tier 3 sub-team establishes a response plan for a student whose behaviors are escalating, but the team members do not consider all stakeholder input and their response is not always timely.	The PBIS Tier 3 sub-team does not establish a timely response plan for a student whose behaviors are escalating.	_____/2
Timeline for Response and Monitoring	The PBIS Tier 3 sub-team meets and begins development of a timely response plan within twenty-four hours of receiving a request for support from a staff member or other stakeholder. The PBIS Tier 3 sub-team puts the response plan in place by the following day or as soon as possible within the week the plan is initiated. The PBIS Tier 3 sub-team monitors the plan frequently and adjusts the plan accordingly based on implementation.	The PBIS Tier 3 sub-team has an inconsistent timeline and monitoring system in place for students needing a Tier 3 timely response plan.	There is no established timeline for response or monitoring in place.	_____/2
Administrator Support	The administration is an active member of this plan and ensures the Tier 3 sub-team members have the resources they need in order to develop and implement a plan in a timely fashion.	The administration is inconsistently involved with the development and implementation of a timely response plan.	The administration is not an active member of the Tier 3 sub-team, therefore making the efforts of the Tier 3 sub-team difficult to implement in a timely fashion.	_____/2
				Total _____/6

(Continued)

(Continued)

Criteria	2 points	1 point	0 points	Score
Marker 5: Establish a Tier 3 Fidelity Check Process				
Fidelity Check Process	The PBIS Tier 3 sub-team has established a fidelity check process to ensure Tier 3 interventions are being implemented with fidelity. The fidelity check process includes the review for students receiving both general education and special education services.	The PBIS Tier 3 sub-team is in the process of developing a fidelity check process for Tier 3 interventions.	No fidelity check process exists for Tier 3 interventions.	_____/2
Multiple Levels	Fidelity of implementation is evaluated at multiple levels (e.g., administration, stakeholder/staff, student, and parent/guardian).	Fidelity of Tier 3 implementation is only evaluated by the administration at this time.	Fidelity of Tier 3 implementation is not evaluated at multiple levels.	_____/2
Staff Fidelity	About 80 percent of the staff comprising both general and special education staff have bought into implementing their role in Tier 3 interventions with fidelity. The PBIS Tier 3 sub-team helps ensure the staff/stakeholders are implementing the Tier 3 interventions with fidelity by frequent check-ins, observations, and creating ongoing opportunities to gather feedback and provide additional supports and trainings.	About 50 percent of the staff have bought into implementing their role in Tier 3 interventions with fidelity. There is no method in place to ensure Tier 3 interventions are being implemented with fidelity by staff in both general education and special education.	The majority of the staff do not believe in the implementation of Tier 3 interventions.	_____/2
				Total _____/6

OVERVIEW OF CATEGORY A T3-MSR RESULTS: TIER 3 PBIS MARKERS

Category A: Scores for Tier 3 Markers	
Category A: Tier 3 PBIS Markers	**What is your score?**
Marker 1: Establish and Operate an Effective PBIS Tier 3 Sub-Team	_____/6
Marker 2: Establish a Culture and Expectation for Supporting All Students	_____/6
Marker 3: Conduct a Tier 3 Resource Inventory	_____/6
Marker 4: Establish a Tier 3 Timely Response Plan	_____/6
Marker 5: Establish a Tier 3 Fidelity Check Process	_____/6
Goal is 80 percent or higher	Total Score: _____/30 = _____ percent

What's Next?

Now that you have learned the necessary Tier 3 markers for creating a strong Tier 3 system foundation, you are ready to design and implement individualized interventions for students in both general education and special education needing Tier 3 interventions. In the next chapter, you will learn how to assess and refine each delivered Tier 3 intervention to include the five characteristics necessary for effectiveness.

Getting Started With Category B— Tier 3 Characteristics

Before we dive into the Tier 3 characteristics, is it very important for us to make clear the intent of this chapter. These characteristics do not replace what is mandated by federal law or need to take place for students receiving special education services; instead, these characteristics are designed to enhance the method by which these intensive interventions are being implemented, delivered, and monitored. Based on our experience, we have noticed a disconnect between the general education and special education systems when it comes to behavior, and therefore we present a team/collaborative approach to evaluate what is offered for Tier 3 interventions to ensure the best outcomes for students. In addition, we highly recommend your experts in behavioral supports and special education are part of these discussions to help ensure the fidelity of design and implementation. However, we do encourage that these plans remain intentional but practical in nature. We have found the number-one reason for failure of Tier 3 interventions to be ineffective implementation by stakeholders because the interventions are too complex. Although experts in behavior may be helping in the design, practitioners who may or may not have similar expertise are the ones implementing these interventions daily, so there needs to be a good balance and compromise in what is doable but continues to produce the best outcomes for students. So to reiterate, Chapter 3 focused on designing a collaborative system for responding to students needing a Tier 3 intervention in a timely manner, and this chapter presents a tool to help audit individualized interventions for students to ensure evidence of key characteristics for success.

This chapter builds on the five Tier 2 intervention characteristics identified in *The PBIS Tier Two Handbook*; in simple terms, all the characteristics identified for Tier 2 interventions still stand as part of a tiered system approach, but at the Tier 3 level, additional characteristics are needed to add layers and intensity of individualized supports. This chapter identifies and describes the five Tier 3 individualized intervention characteristics that need to be present in each Tier 3 intervention offered at your school, guides you through an assessment of your current state, presents challenges from the field with practical solutions, and prompts reflection based on Tier 3 assessment data about next-step actions to move your system from current state to desired future—Gold Positive Behavior Interventions and Supports (PBIS) Champion Model. For a school functioning at the Gold PBIS Champion level, however, the ultimate goal is to ensure that *every student needing a Tier 3 intervention* can demonstrate evidence of these five Tier 3 characteristics, and an intervention is designed by name and by need for each individual student. Specifically, this chapter is designed to help you develop, implement, and monitor the Tier 3 interventions offered at your school using the five Tier 3 characteristics as a guide.

Note

Something very important to consider as you begin this chapter is that there is no one-size-fits-all framework for a Tier 3 intervention; rather, it depends on the student. Often, case study examples are presented in the research—consider these a guide to the structure of the intervention.

TIP: *As you read through each characteristic, have in mind a student who has needed or is receiving a Tier 3 intervention; you can use that example as a guide as you go through each marker.* Write down a brief description of the student you will be using as a reference as you read through the characteristics:

_____

_____

_____

_____

_____

CRITICAL TAKEAWAYS

- In Chapter 3, you began the hard work of building a Tier 3 behavior system designed to support the implementation of effective Tier 3 interventions.
- In this chapter, you will learn how to establish and implement the five characteristics essential for each Tier 3 intervention offered at your school.
- We recommend that any Tier 3 intervention offered at your school include evidence for all five characteristics in this chapter.
- The five characteristics in this chapter are designed to help you evaluate the level of fidelity and practicality in the Tier 3 interventions currently offered at your school, and to help you establish new or enhance current Tier 3 interventions based on the need and data of individualized students.
- In the previous chapter, we asked you to view the markers from a systems-level lens. For the purpose of this chapter, it is important to evaluate each of these five characteristics using a Tier 3 intervention–specific student lens (e.g., evaluate, enhance, or develop the five characteristics for each Tier 3 intervention offered at your school).
- This is in no way a replacement for special education Individualized Education Program (IEP) Tier 3 characteristics. This is a guide for the PBIS Tier 3 sub-team to utilize and help the overall Tier 3 system at the school. However, it is important that the characteristics in place for special education students on an intensive behavior plan include the five characteristics described in this chapter in order to ensure full implementation of an individualized intervention.

TIP: Utilize school- or district-level staff with behavior and special education expertise as you develop, enhance, and refine effective Tier 3 interventions at your school using these five characteristics as a guide.

So what are the five Tier 3 characteristics? The five characteristics are as follows:

Characteristic 1: Conduct a Student History Review

Characteristic 2: Conduct an Environment Review

Characteristic 3: Identify Function and Provide Replacement Skills

Characteristic 4: Present Evidence of a Practical Plan/Schedule

Characteristic 5: Plan for Progress Monitoring/Communication

TIER 3 CHARACTERISTICS

A strong Tier 3 PBIS system that supports the implementation of effective Tier 3 interventions will have evidence of a strong Tier 1 and Tier 2 PBIS foundation firmly in place and all Tier 3 markers (Chapter 3) established. Investing in these systems will allow for additional resources at your school to assist students needing intensive, individualized plans.

For each Tier 3 intervention offered at your school, you need to ensure each of the five Tier 3 characteristics is present. These five Tier 3 characteristics can best be captured and assessed through the completion of the Tier 3 Intervention Snapshot Interview (a full version is available at the end of this chapter).

TIP: Conduct a Tier 3 Intervention Snapshot Interview for each Tier 3 intervention offered at your school. (For the purpose of starting this process, select one general education and one special education Tier 3 intervention to review, refine, or create using these markers as a guide.)

This interview process and tool was designed to gather evidence for Tier 3 intervention implementation through observations and evidence of these characteristics. It provides a snapshot view of each Tier 3 individualized intervention in place at a school based on input from implementers, evidence presented, and Tier 3 individualized student data. This process of designing, implementing, and collecting evidence for each of these five Tier 3 characteristics should, at minimum, be conducted for each student receiving an intensive individualized intervention and be used as a tool throughout the school year to ensure the Tier 3 intervention designed and offered for each individual student is being followed as intended.

Who should complete the Tier 3 Intervention Snapshot Interview?

To obtain accurate baseline information for each Tier 3 individualized intervention offered at your school, the PBIS Tier 3 sub-team should complete a form for each student receiving support at this level.

Note

This should only be a small handful of students if you are implementing the tiered system of supports as designed in the Champion Model. The full version of the Tier 3 Intervention Snapshot Interview is available at the end of this chapter. This Tier 3 Intervention Snapshot Interview is designed to give your team additional characteristics to consider. Sometimes teams are in a desperate and emotionally driven state when students escalate to this level of support, so it is important to continue expanding on what has already been done with fidelity in order to get to a solution. We hear often, "We tried this; we tried that," but no evidence exists to support it. Also, it is important to document all that has been tried with evidence in the student record in order to demonstrate what the school has implemented. These records may be used to evaluate the need for additional services, possible alternative programming/placement, or discipline, or to provide relevant information for students in case they move from your school or district.

How will the Tier 3 Intervention Snapshot Interview data be used?

You will use the results of the Tier 3 Intervention Snapshot Interview to perform a gap analysis to gain a better understanding of each of your Tier 3 interventions in relation to the five Tier 3 characteristics. You will calculate your points for each of the five characteristics and receive an overall score for each Tier 3 intervention offered at your school.

Note

For the purpose of Gold PBIS Champion Model status, you will need to demonstrate the On Target level (described in the Scoring Guide) with evidence for one general education and one special education Tier 3 intervention offered at your school. However, as mentioned, best practice would be to have all five Tier 3 characteristics in place for each Tier 3 intervention offered at your school.

TIER 3 INTERVENTION SNAPSHOT INTERVIEW SCORING GUIDE

On Target	8–10 points
Making Progress	4–7 points
Needs Improvement	0–3 points

Evidence of a strong Tier 3 intervention is an overall Tier 3 Intervention Snapshot Interview score in the 8–10 **On Target** point range. This Tier 3 intervention interview data should be used as another valuable information stream to inform next steps. Therefore, it is important that objective responses are provided. The results from the Tier 3 Intervention Snapshot Interview are one measure to show attainment of Tier 3 Gold PBIS Champion Model status. Remember, you will need to demonstrate evidence of a Tier 3 snapshot for one general education student and one special education student in need of Tier 3 individualized intervention at the On Target level, meaning the five Tier 3 characteristics have been considered and implemented in each individualized plan.

A first step toward developing a Tier 3 Gold PBIS Champion Model School is to assess the current state of your own system; then identify next-step, high-leverage actions based on data analysis, taking into consideration not only data from your Tier 3 Intervention Snapshot Interviews but the results of your five critical Tier 3 Markers Scoring Rubric (T3-MSR) (Category A—Chapter 3).

The next section of this chapter guides you through a quick assessment of each of the five Tier 3 characteristics, provides you with the opportunity to reflect on the current state and next steps for each Tier 3 intervention at your school, and presents challenges and practical solutions from the field.

TIP: Go through each of the five characteristics for one general education and one special education student receiving a Tier 3 intervention at your school.

In this section, you will evaluate your current Tier 3 interventions using the five Tier 3 characteristics as a guide. The items from the Tier 3 Intervention Snapshot Interview are divided into the five characteristics.

TIP: As you go through each of the five Tier 3 characteristics in this section, identify one general education and one special education student receiving a Tier 3 intervention to begin this process. When your Tier 3 sub-team can demonstrate evidence for each of the five Tier 3 characteristics for each of these identified Tier 3 interventions at your school, go through this same process with a critical eye for any additional students receiving Tier 3 interventions offered at your school. Use this template to help organize which Tier 3 interventions you have reviewed using this process.

C = Characteristic

Tier 3 Intervention Student Name	*C1—In place **or** Not in place*	*C2—In place **or** Not in place*	*C3—In place **or** Not in place*	*C4—In place **or** Not in place*	*C5—In place **or** Not in place*
General Education Student Tier 3 Intervention:					
Special Education Student Tier 3 Intervention:					

TIME TO BEGIN: TIER 3 CHARACTERISTICS

Characteristic 1
Conduct a Student History Review
The PBIS Tier 3 sub-team has conducted a thorough student history review prior to establishing a Tier 3 intervention. This can include but is not limited to medical history, general education history, special education history if applicable, academic and behavior intervention documentation, contact with previous school, and teacher, program, home, and other factors. Note: For a special education student, work with the school psychologist and the IEP team to gather all pertinent information.

Assessing Our Current State:
Where Are We in Relation to Characteristic 1?

Section of the Tier 3 Snapshot Interview

Tier 3 Characteristic	Evidence of Characteristic	Points 0—Not in Place 1—In Progress 2—In Place With Evidence
Characteristic 1: Conduct a Student History Review	• Medical history documentation • Previous academic and behavior intervention documentation • General education history • Special education history if applicable • Contact with previous school, teacher, program, home factors, etc. • Parent or guardian collaboration, survey input, etc. • Other information to consider: _____ _____ _____ _____	Total: ____/2

What actions should we take to move this Tier 3 intervention closer to target on the Tier 3 characteristic?

_____

_____

_____

_____

_____

_____

_____

_____

_____

_____

◈◈◈

FROM THE FIELD: CHARACTERISTIC 1

Challenge: The PBIS Tier 3 sub-team members did not have a list of questions to consider as they were evaluating or creating a new Tier 3 intervention for a student in need. This was leading to a lot of discussion and no action.

◈◈◈

How would you address this challenge?

_____

_____

_____

_____

_____

_____

_____

_____

◈◈◈

Practical solution: The PBIS Tier 3 sub-team members combined their most commonly asked questions to consider into a checklist to evaluate against or use to help enhance or establish a Tier 3 intervention. This checklist held them accountable for having all available information on the student present before making any Tier 3 intervention decisions.

Tool/resource used: Student History Review Checklist

Student History Review Checklist

☐ Is the student in special education or general education?

☐ If special education, does the student have a behavior support plan and behavior goal? Has a recent IEP been held?

☐ Is the student taking medication?

☐ Does the school have a release of information from the doctor?

☐ Is the function of the behavior identified?

☐ Is the environment changed at all (intensified structure)?

☐ Are academics changed?

☐ Is family connected/supportive?

☐ Is mental health connected?

☐ Are wraparound services available?

☐ How much time and human resources is it taking to stabilize the student?

☐ How often is this intervention monitored?

☐ Other possible questions to consider:

_____

_____

_____

_____

Characteristic 2 **Conduct an Environment Review**		

An environment review requires the Tier 3 sub-team to consider the environment in which the identified student is receiving instruction. In cases where the student is receiving special education services, an evaluation of services is conducted with the appropriate special education team members who can help with environmental decisions. An adjustment or modification of the environment is considered as part of the Tier 3 intervention developed for the student.

Assessing Our Current State: Where Are We in Relation to Characteristic 2?

Section of the Tier 3 Snapshot Interview

Tier 3 Characteristic	Evidence of Characteristic	Points 0—Not in Place 1—In Progress 2—In Place With Evidence
Characteristic 2: Conduct an Environment Review	• Interview data • Observation data • IEP review notes if applicable • Sensory considerations • Other information to consider: _____ _____ _____ _____	Total: _____/2

What actions should we take to move this Tier 3 intervention closer to target on the Tier 3 characteristic?

_____

_____

_____

_____

_____

FROM THE FIELD: CHARACTERISTIC 2

Challenge: The PBIS Tier 3 sub-team members were having a challenging time reviewing the effectiveness of a Tier 3 intervention currently in progress. Their biggest challenge was how to creatively take environmental factors into consideration while developing the plan but continue to allow the student to have access to his education. They were confused about what data to utilize to make these decisions. In addition, the process for adjusting the environment as part of the environment review was different for special education and general education students.

How would you address this challenge?

_____

_____

_____

_____

_____

_____

_____

_____

_____

_____

Practical solution: The PBIS Tier 3 sub-team decided to conduct an interview/observation with the student in the school environment to help make decisions about whether or not the Tier 3 intervention was designed for this student's success.

Tool/resource used: Student Interview/Observation Form: Environment Review Form

Student Interview/Observation Form: Environment Review Form			
Student Name:			
Interviewee/Observer Name:			
Date:			
Student Interview/ Input Section	Observation 1 notes Time of day: _____	Observation 2 notes Time of day: _____	Observation 3 notes Time of day: _____
What is your current learning environment?			
What is challenging for you given your learning environment?			
What time of day is the most challenging? Why?			
What can be adjusted in your environment to support your learning?			
What would your ideal learning environment look like?			

Characteristic 3
Identify Function and Provide Replacement Skills

The function of the behavior (e.g., to avoid, to get something, sensory, social attention) is identified as a guide to develop the instructional replacement skill component of the Tier 3 intervention. Note: If you are reviewing a special education behavior support plan as a Tier 3 intervention, make sure the function is identified and there is a teaching component to help the student gain replacement behaviors as part of the behavior support plan or behavior IEP goals.

Assessing Our Current State: Where Are We in Relation to Characteristic 3?

Section of the Tier 3 Snapshot Interview

Tier 3 Characteristic	Evidence of Characteristic	Points 0—Not in Place 1—In Progress 2—In Place With Evidence
Characteristic 3: Identify Function and Provide Replacement Skills	• Behavior lessons • Corrective feedback schedule • Social stories • Method of how function was identified Other information to consider: _____ _____ _____ _____	Total: ____/2

⇜⇝

What actions should we take to move this Tier 3 intervention to target on the Tier 3 characteristic?

_____

_____

_____

_____

_____

_____

_____

⇜⇝

FROM THE FIELD: CHARACTERISTIC 3

Challenge: The PBIS Tier 3 sub-team members did not feel as if they were able to identify the function of a student's behavior without a behavior expert on their team. The school psychologist was asked to be part of the team to help with the identification and design of the intervention to include an instructional component. Note: This in no way means the school psychologist was charged with conducting a functional analysis assessment for every student needing Tier 3 intervention supports; it just means that the school psychologist's expertise was utilized.

How would you address this challenge?

_____

_____

_____

_____

_____

_____

_____

_____

_____

_____

_____

Practical solution: With the help of the school psychologist, the PBIS Tier 3 sub-team developed a simple guide to cross-check existing plans or general education Tier 3 intervention plan development to ensure the identification of the function, evidence to demonstrate the reason for this perceived function, and a method of providing an instructional component aligned with the plan.

Tool/resource used: Replacement Behavior Guide

Replacement Behavior Guide

Student Name:

_____

General Education or Special Education:

_____

If special education, does the student have a behavior support plan?

_____

Perceived function of behavior: to avoid, to get something, sensory, social attention

_____

Evidence for perceived function:

_____

Recommended replacement behavior skill:

_____

Frequency of replacement behavior skill taught:

_____

Dates instruction has been provided:

_____

Who will teach replacement behavior daily:

_____

Resources needed to teach replacement behavior:

_____

Other important information:

_____

How can we refine the intervention if we are missing any of these components?

_____

_____

_____

_____

Characteristic 4 **Present Evidence of a Practical Plan/Schedule**	
A practical plan/schedule is designed to help all stakeholders involved with the Tier 3 intervention understand how to implement a complex individualized intervention for a student. Some stakeholders may not have had intensive behavioral intervention background training, and therefore the plan needs to be assessed for doability.	

Assessing Our Current State: Where Are We in Relation to Characteristic 4?

Section of the Tier 3 Snapshot Interview

Tier 3 Characteristic	Evidence of Characteristic	Points 0—Not in Place 1—In Progress 2—In Place With Evidence
Characteristic 4: Present Evidence of a Practical Plan/Schedule	• System for organizing Tier 3 interventions • Structured schedule • Individualized plan with identified stakeholder roles • Behavior support plan • Other information to consider: _____ _____ _____ _____	Total: ____/2

❧❦

What actions should we take to move our school closer to target on the Tier 3 characteristic?

_____

_____

_____

_____

_____

❧❦

FROM THE FIELD: CHARACTERISTIC 4

Challenge: The stakeholders involved with the Tier 3 interventions at the school were having a difficult time keeping track of exactly what to do with each Tier 3 intervention plan they had at the school. They did not always have access to the more detailed Tier 3 intervention plans during supervision or implementation of the Tier 3 intervention.

How would you address this challenge?

_____

_____

_____

_____

_____

_____

_____

_____

_____

_____

Practical solution: The PBIS Tier 3 sub-team decided stakeholders needed a method to refer to in a practical way to ensure practicality of Tier 3 intervention implementation. They decided to develop Tier 3 Intervention Cheat Sheet student index cards that they laminated and put on a ring for stakeholders to have access to at all times in case the behaviors escalated and they did not have access to the more detailed Tier 3 intervention plans.

Tool/resource used: Tier 3 Intervention Cheat Sheet Student Template (opposite page)

Extra tool/resource used: Structured Day Schedule Plan Example (pages 78–79)

Tier 3 Intervention Cheat Sheet Student Template

Name of student:

_____

Reason for the intervention:

_____

_____

Behavior triggers:

_____

Steps to take if behavior observed:

_____

_____

Special schedule:

_____

Special notes:

_____

_____

_____

_____

Structured Day Schedule Plan Example
Week of November 17–December 15

Before School

- Student is to check in the office to pick up Check-In Check-Out (CICO) folder; administrator reviews structured day schedule and daily goals with student.
- Student gets escorted to class with the supervision of the home volunteer or designated school personnel (who will ensure he turns in homework or classwork not completed from the day before and understands the given task).
- Classroom teacher teaches class as usual (documents on CICO form if sees minor misbehaviors).
- Suggestion: Student is to fill out the CICO chart at the end of the day so that he is not thrown off by a rating he does not like throughout the day but it will still be documented and parent/guardian will also know of the behavior that led to that rating.

After Morning Recess

- Student comes to the office after morning recess and is escorted to class by home volunteer or designated school personnel (who will ensure he understands task he has to complete in class).

After Lunch Recess

- Student comes to the office after lunch recess and is escorted to class by home volunteer or designated school personnel (who will ensure he understands task he has to complete in class).

End of Day and After School

- Designated school personnel or home volunteer will ensure student has incomplete work folder and homework ready to take home to complete.
- Parent will pick up student after school daily (student will not be walking home during this intervention).

Important note to consider throughout the day: RED ZONE (aka designated location with structured assignments)

- If the teacher notices a student is disrupting teaching or about to engage in attention-seeking behavior with the teacher (power struggle), the teacher sends the student with a red folder to the office or makes a phone call to the office with a selected code for someone to come help with the situation.
- If the student is at the point where he has to be removed, he will complete the following structured assignments (and others as determined by the teacher): read an Accelerated Reader (AR) book (take notes, pass a quiz), do Spatial Temporal (ST) Math (forty minutes), complete a Lexia online literacy program (forty minutes), play a math facts game, write an essay on appropriate behavior, finish any incomplete work, etc.).

Progress Monitoring (Fill out and track the number of times in each day the student got in the RED ZONE.)

S = Student   T = Teacher   P = Parent   A = Administrator   O = Other

Dates	How many times did the student get in the RED ZONE?	Did we follow the plan with fidelity today? Yes (Y) or No (N)				
Week		S	T	P	A	O
Monday						
Tuesday						
Wednesday						
Thursday						
Friday						
Week		S	T	P	A	O
Monday						
Tuesday						
Wednesday						
Thursday						
Friday						
Week		S	T	P	A	O
Monday						
Tuesday						
Wednesday						
Thursday						
Friday						
Week		S	T	P	A	O
Monday						
Tuesday						
Wednesday						
Thursday						
Friday						

Note: This component of the Structured Day Schedule Plan meets the requirement for the fifth Tier 3 characteristic, Plan for Progress Monitoring/Communication, which we will address next.

<table>
<tr><td colspan="2" align="center">**Characteristic 5**
Plan for Progress Monitoring/Communication</td></tr>
<tr><td colspan="2">The Tier 3 intervention includes a progress monitoring and communication component to the plan. All stakeholders are aware of how to monitor the implementation and communicate with each other as needed based on the effectiveness of the plan. The progress monitoring instructions are easy to follow and can be accessed by all team members who need to ensure they are doing it correctly.</td></tr>
</table>

Assessing Our Current State: Where Are We in Relation to Characteristic 5?

Section of the Tier 3 Snapshot Interview

Tier 3 Characteristic	Evidence of Characteristic	Points 0—Not in Place 1—In Progress 2—In Place With Evidence
Characteristic 5: Plan for Progress Monitoring/ Communication	• System for communicating Tier 3 intervention progress • Clear instructions • Dates established for the review • Evidence of all stakeholder understanding • Other information to consider _____ _____ _____ _____	Total: ____/2

What actions should we take to move our school closer to target on the Tier 3 characteristic?

_____

_____

_____

_____

_____

_____

_____

_____

_____

_____

FROM THE FIELD: CHARACTERISTIC 5

Challenge: The PBIS Tier 3 sub-team members needed a frame to help organize the monitoring and communication portion of the Tier 3 interventions offered. They wanted an easier way to organize each Tier 3 intervention offered at the school.

How would you address this challenge?

_____

_____

_____

_____

_____

_____

_____

_____

Practical solution: The PBIS Tier 3 sub-team created a Tier 3 Intervention at a Glance document to help provide a reference to the who, what, how, and measured components of every Tier 3 intervention offered. This held them accountable for documenting and deciding who was in charge of monitoring and communicating based on the Tier 3 intervention plan.

Tool/resource used: Tier 3 Intervention at a Glance: Structured Day Sample (opposite page)

Notes

_____

_____

_____

_____

_____

_____

_____

_____

_____

_____

Tier 3 Intervention At a Glance: Structured Day Sample

Who?

Student not responding to Tier 1 and Tier 2 interventions (e.g., at least one major incident a day that requires two or three adults to help stabilize). Administrator, staff, and teachers involved with implementing the Structured Day Schedule with fidelity.

What?

Structured Day Schedule: special schedule developed to meet the individual needs of the student and support success throughout the school day academically and behaviorally.

How?

Staff designated to supervise and work with student during designated time throughout the day. All involved communicate with each other and student daily. Student receives daily lessons and/or intentional precorrections on how to demonstrate appropriate behaviors to meet individual goals.

Measured?

Monitored by individualized academic and behavior SMART (Strategic and Specific, Measurable, Attainable/Achievable, Results-Oriented and Relevant, and Time-Bound) goals daily. The schedule is progress monitored and adjusted as needed by PBIS Tier 3 sub-team that meets to review at least weekly. Administrator monitors and takes daily pulse and ensures fidelity of the schedule. Decide as a team every ten days of implementation with fidelity if student will continue on the schedule or needs additional supports.

OVERVIEW OF CATEGORY B
TIER 3 INTERVENTION SNAPSHOT
INTERVIEW RESULTS: TIER 3 CHARACTERISTICS

Tier 3 Intervention Snapshot Interview

Name of the student receiving the Tier 3 intervention: _____

Special Education or General Education: _____

Tier 3 Characteristic	Evidence of Characteristic (Include your evidence examples below for each characteristic)	Points 0—Not in Place 1—In Progress 2—In Place With Evidence
Characteristic 1: Conduct a Student History Review		Characteristic 1 point total: ____/2
Characteristic 2: Conduct an Environment Review		Characteristic 2 point total: ____/2
Characteristic 3: Identify Function and Provide Replacement Skills		Characteristic 3 point total: ____/2

Characteristic 4: Provide Evidence of a Practical Plan/ Schedule		Characteristic 4 point total: ____/2
Characteristic 5: Plan for Progress Monitoring/ Communication		Characteristic 5 point total: ____/2
Additional observations:		Total Score: ____/10 Overall Scoring Guide:

Overall Scoring Guide:

On Target	8–10 points
Making Progress	4–7 points
Needs Improvement	0–3 points

Getting Started With Category C— Tier 3 Academic and Behavior SMART Goals and the Work of the PBIS Tier 3 Sub-Team

This section of the book focuses on the continued development of a Positive Behavior Interventions and Supports (PBIS) Champion Model System at the Gold Level; specifically, this chapter will allow you to establish Tier 3 academic and behavior goals and the actions of a school's PBIS Tier 3 sub-team to support this work. How can you monitor for effectiveness of the Tier 3 interventions offered without goals present? You can't. Your Tier 3 sub-team must set goals that are monitored to see if the Tier 3 interventions provided are working. One critical role of the Tier 3 sub-team is to set and evaluate these Tier 3 intervention goals on at least a weekly basis. Reviewing goals and progress should be a standing agenda item in every Tier 3 sub-team meeting. It is important to note there are two levels of goal setting: *Level 1* goals are the **collective** Tier 3 intervention academic and behavior goals (e.g., goals based on the common areas students are working on academically and behaviorally to see if the majority of the students receiving a Tier 3 intervention are responding and meeting their collective goals); *Level 2* goals are the **individual** student Tier 3 intervention goals (e.g., individual goals based on the needs of each individual student; therefore, if the Tier 3 intervention collective goals are not met, students who are responding and making progress are not missed).

The Tier 3 intervention goals provided in this section are Level 2 goal examples, which are individual in nature. It is critical that the Tier 3 sub-team review these goals with up-to-date data for each Tier 3 intervention offered at the school during weekly Tier 3 sub-team meetings. This will allow for modifications and adjustments as necessary based on data and stakeholder input.

For the purpose of attaining Gold Level PBIS Champion Model status, your school needs to demonstrate effectiveness of one Tier 3 intervention offered at your school in general education and one offered at your school in special education. Data evidence of meeting academic and behavior SMART (Strategic and Specific, Measurable, Attainable/Achievable, Results-Oriented and Relevant, and Time-Bound) goals at the individual level for each of the identified students (one general education student and one special education student) should be demonstrated.

TIP: It is important for us to note that best practice is that you have established SMART goals aligned for every student receiving a Tier 3 intervention offered at your school. As your Tier 3 sub-team builds its capacity to design and monitor Tier 3 interventions and goals effectively, it is recommended that you develop individualized academic and behavior goals for each student needing a Tier 3 intervention at your school.

Note

We receive many questions asking why academic goals are connected to each Tier 3 intervention. In short, we believe that everything we do social-emotionally is to also support the academic success of each student; therefore, it is necessary to make a connection between academics and behavior in the goals.

Note

If you do not have any general education or special education students in need of a Tier 3 intervention, then you just have to demonstrate that with evidence. For example, some Gold Level schools have maybe one case at a time since their systems are responding to their tiered levels of support.

CRITICAL TAKEAWAYS

- In Chapter 3, you learned how to develop a Tier 3 behavior system, and in Chapter 4, you learned about the Tier 3 characteristics necessary within each Tier 3 intervention provided at your school.
- In this chapter, you will learn how to establish and monitor academic and behavior SMART goals for each Tier 3 intervention provided at your school. Essentially, you are evaluating the effectiveness of your Tier 3 behavior system.
- We recommend these SMART goals be monitored by the Tier 3 PBIS sub-team on (at minimum) a weekly basis. It is essential to review the data from these Tier 3 interventions to determine which students are in need of additional supports for their academic and behavioral success. For special education students, this process is in addition to any Individualized Education Program (IEP) review of behavior goals aligned with formal behavior support plans in place.
- To reiterate, in Chapter 3, you learned how to build the foundation to support the Tier 3 interventions provided at your school; in Chapter 4, you learned how to design and evaluate essential characteristics necessary for effective Tier 3 interventions; and in this chapter, you will learn how to establish and monitor SMART goals for every Tier 3 intervention provided at your school.

So why have an academic and behavior SMART goal for each Tier 3 intervention at your school?

Tier 3 interventions are designed to help students receive individualized behavioral supports needed to access their education. So ultimately, improving or maintaining academics for students receiving Tier 3 interventions is one strong indicator of whether or not the implemented Tier 3 intervention is effective. Additionally, having academic and behavior SMART goals aligned with each Tier 3 intervention will help the PBIS Tier 3 sub-team monitor progress on at least a weekly basis and share this information with stakeholders.

A school must demonstrate positive change in academic and behavioral outcomes aligned with one general education and one special education Tier 3 intervention provided at the school to become a Gold Level PBIS Champion Model School. Gold Level schools must also have the preceding tiers (Tier 1—Bronze Level and Tier 2—Silver Level) firmly established while also achieving academic and behavior goals in the current tier (Tier 3—Gold Level):

- Tier 1: The Bronze Level requires at least one **School-Wide** academic and behavior SMART goal to be established and achieved (see *The PBIS Tier One Handbook* as a reference).
- Tier 2: The Silver Level requires that the Tier 1 goals are met with at least one collective **Targeted/At-Risk** Tier 2 intervention academic and behavior SMART goal established and achieved for students.
- Tier 3: The Gold Level requires that the Tier 1 and Tier 2 goals are met and **Individualized** academic and behavior SMART goals are established and achieved for at least one student in general education and one student in special education who are not responding to Tier 1 and Tier 2 interventions.

So what is a Tier 3 intervention academic goal? A Tier 3 academic goal is an individualized intervention academic SMART goal drafted by the PBIS Tier 3 sub-team based on individualized academic data of the students receiving Tier 3 interventions.

So what is a Tier 3 intervention behavior goal? A Tier 3 behavior goal is an individualized intervention SMART goal drafted by the PBIS Tier 3 sub-team based on individualized behavioral data of the students receiving a Tier 3 intervention at the school.

The PBIS Champion Model uses multiple data sources to establish at least one Tier 3 intervention academic goal and one Tier 3 intervention behavior goal, develops actions directly aligned toward achieving established goals, executes the actions, then monitors and communicates progress toward achieving the goals.

In this chapter, we will provide a series of questions for you to consider as you reflect on your Tier 3 systems, an action plan template to support future work, and a Tier 3 academic and behavior goals questionnaire. The questionnaire should be used to assess the current state of your selected tier individualized intervention relative to academic and behavior goals (one offered for a special education student and one offered for a general education student). The action plan template can be used to help plan, execute, and monitor next-step, high-leverage systems work. The important aspect of Category C is that your system establishes at least one general education and one special education Tier 3 intervention academic goal and one behavior goal that includes specific indicators of success, develops actions directly aligned to those goals, executes the actions, then monitors progress toward goal attainment. This should be a focus for the PBIS Tier 3 sub-team—to lead this work.

Who should complete the questionnaire? The PBIS Tier 3 sub-team should complete the questionnaire. If you do not have a PBIS Tier 3 sub-team established just yet, the PBIS team or the school leadership team should complete the questionnaire.

Tier 3 Academic and Behavior Goals Questionnaire		
Questions to Consider	**Academic** **Yes or No**	**Behavioral** **Yes or No**
1. Does our school have a PBIS Tier 3 sub-team that reviews Tier 3 intervention academic/behavioral data for both general education and special education students?		
2. Does our PBIS Tier 3 sub-team meet at least weekly to review Tier 3 intervention academic/behavioral data for both general education and special education students?		
3. Does our PBIS Tier 3 sub-team have access to Tier 3 intervention academic/behavioral data for both general education and special education students?		
4. Has our PBIS Tier 3 sub-team established at least one Tier 3 intervention academic/behavior SMART goal based on assessed need for both general education and special education students?		
5. Can every PBIS Tier 3 sub-team member at our school articulate our Tier 3 intervention academic/behavior SMART goals for both general education and special education students?		
6. Does our school have a process to monitor progress toward meeting our established Tier 3 intervention academic/ behavior SMART goals for both general education and special education students?		
7. Does our school have a plan to communicate progress made on Tier 3 intervention academic/behavior SMART goals to our staff and stakeholders for both general education and special education students?		
8. Does our school PBIS Tier 3 sub-team use an agenda that focuses discussion on our Tier 3 academic/behavior SMART goals for both general education and special education students?		

TIER 3 INTERVENTION ACADEMIC AND BEHAVIOR GOALS: ACTIONS TO CONSIDER BASED ON DATA ANALYSIS

- A PBIS Tier 3 sub-team is established that reviews Tier 3 intervention academic and behavioral data.
- The PBIS Tier 3 sub-team meets at least weekly to review Tier 3 academic and behavioral data.
- The administration or a selected Tier 3 intervention lead provides the Tier 3 sub-team with access to Tier 3 intervention academic and behavioral data and prepares and provides reports requested by the PBIS Tier 3 sub-team at every meeting. *Note: The administration supports this lead member with resources and protected time to organize Tier 3 intervention information.*
- The PBIS Tier 3 sub-team develops at least one Tier 3 academic and behavior SMART goal (including indicators of success) based on Tier 3 data and stakeholder input.
- The PBIS Tier 3 sub-team regularly (every staff meeting) has a designated time to educate and update the rest of staff on Tier 3 intervention progress.
- The PBIS Tier 3 sub-team establishes a process and schedule to monitor the Tier 3 intervention academic and behavior goals for both general education and special education students.
- Staff build their knowledge of the *why* and *how* of implementing Tier 3 interventions in support of achieving individualized intervention academic and behavior SMART goals.

Analyze your Tier 3 intervention academic and behavior goals questionnaire data. What did the data tell you? Based on the information gained from this analysis and the suggested actions to consider, what next-step or high-leverage actions will your PBIS Tier 3 sub-team take in support of the work—which is to establish at least one Tier 3 intervention academic and behavior SMART goal that includes specific indicators of success, develop directly aligned actions to accomplish those goals, execute actions, and monitor progress toward goal attainment for both general education and special education students?

Actions:

For each action, state when the action will start, the person(s) responsible, evidence of the action, and the target completion date. As you monitor these actions, include the date as each is completed.

Action	Timeline (week and day to start action)	Person(s) Responsible	Evidence	Target Completion Date (week/day)	Actual Completion Date (week/day)
1.					
2.					
3.					
4.					

If your system has already established a Tier 3 intervention academic goal and a Tier 3 intervention behavior goal for both general education and special education students, then use the following tools ("Comparing Our Tier 3 Intervention Academic Goal With SMART Goal Characteristics" and "Comparing Our Tier 3 Intervention Behavior Goal with SMART Goal Characteristics") to compare your goals with SMART goal criteria. If your system does not have Tier 3 intervention goals set in one or both of these areas (academic and behavior), use the SMART criteria to establish your goals.

Note

Special education students may already have established academic and behavior goals established as part of their behavior support plan or IEP, so feel free to utilize the same goals if they are SMART goals as your measure. The example provided in this chapter is for a general education student receiving a Tier 3 intervention.

COMPARING OUR TIER 3 INTERVENTION ACADEMIC GOAL WITH SMART GOAL CHARACTERISTICS

Does our academic goal have each of the following characteristics?

Strategic and **S**pecific

Measurable

Attainable/**A**chievable

Results-Oriented and **R**elevant

Time-Bound

SAMPLE: General Education Student Academic SMART Goal:

Comparing a Tier 3 Intervention Academic Goal With SMART Goal Characteristics

SMART Goal Characteristics	Our Tier 3 Intervention Academic Goal: Write your Tier 3 academic goal.
	By the end of the fourth week, the student will complete at least 25 percent of weekly assignments on average per week for four weeks compared to the beginning of his individualized intervention.
	Note: Baseline data prior to the individualized intervention is 0 percent assignments completed per week. This SMART goal is a general education example. For special education Tier 3 interventions, please work with your IEP team to write and decide on SMART goals.
Strategic and Specific	*By the end of the fourth week, the student will complete at least 25 percent of weekly assignments on average per week for four weeks compared to the beginning of his individualized intervention.*
	Research has found there is a correlation between academic difficulties and acting-out behavior. Students who are suspended or expelled from school tend to do worse academically over time than students who do not struggle academically. We believe the more proactive we are in helping students academically, the greater the likelihood that we will increase positive academic outcomes for our students.
Measurable	*The four weeks prior to the individualized student intervention, assignments completed per week are compared to assignments completed four weeks after the intervention.*
	We have the baseline data (0 percent assignments completed per week) and a data collection system that will give us the end of the four-week data.
Attainable/ Achievable	*Note: Baseline data prior to the individualized intervention is 0 percent assignments completed per week.*
	We know our baseline data and believe with the implementation of an individualized intervention, a higher percentage, at least 25 percent of assignments completed on average per week after the four weeks, is attainable. The daily check-in and monitoring system will help the student stay accountable for his academic performance.
Results-Oriented and Relevant	*Results-Oriented: At least 25 percent of weekly assignments on average per week will be completed.*
	Relevant: A Multi-Tiered System of Supports (MTSS) is a framework designed to help provide tiered levels of support behaviorally and academically for all students. This includes teaching behavior similar to academics and providing individualized support based on student data and needs.
Time-Bound	*By the end of the four weeks of intervention.*

PRACTICE: Use the blank template below with your PBIS Tier 3 sub-team to establish your Tier 3 intervention academic goal.

SMART Goal Characteristics	Our Tier 3 Intervention Academic Goal: Write your Tier 3 intervention academic goal.
Strategic and Specific	Write the portion of your Tier 3 intervention academic goal evidencing that it is strategic and specific.
Measurable	Write the portion of your Tier 3 intervention academic goal evidencing that it is measurable.
Attainable/ Achievable	Explain why you believe your Tier 3 intervention academic goal is attainable/ achievable.
Results-Oriented and Relevant	Write the portion of your Tier 3 intervention academic goal with evidence that it is results-oriented and relevant.
Time-Bound	Write the portion of your Tier 3 intervention academic goal evidencing that it is time-bound.

The final version of our Tier 3 intervention academic SMART goal is . . .

_____

_____

_____

_____

_____

_____

_____

_____

_____

_____

_____

COMPARING OUR TIER 3 INTERVENTION BEHAVIOR GOAL WITH SMART GOAL CHARACTERISTICS

Does our behavior goal have each of the following characteristics?

Strategic and **S**pecific

Measurable

Attainable/**A**chievable

Results-Oriented and **R**elevant

Time-Bound

A comparison of an example Tier 3 intervention behavior goal with SMART goal characteristics follows on the next page. There is also a blank template to help you establish your own Tier 3 intervention behavior goal.

SAMPLE: General Education Student Intervention Behavior SMART Goal:

Comparing a Tier 3 Intervention Behavior Goal With SMART Goal Characteristics

SMART Goal Characteristics	Our Tier 3 Intervention Behavior Goal:
	Write your Tier 3 behavior goal.
	By the end of the fourth week of participating in the individualized intervention, there will be a decrease in number of suspension days for the student by 50 percent compared to the beginning of the individualized intervention.
	Note: Baseline: three suspension days a week. This SMART goal is a general education example. For special education Tier 3 interventions, please work with your IEP team to write and decide on SMART goals.
Strategic and Specific	*By the end of the fourth week of participating in the individualized intervention, there will be a decrease in number of suspension days for the student by 50 percent when compared to the baseline suspension data four weeks prior to beginning the individualized intervention.*
	Research has found that students who are suspended or expelled from school tend to do worse behaviorally over time than students who comply with school rules. We believe the more proactive we are in teaching skills the students are lacking, the greater the likelihood we will increase positive behavioral outcomes for our students.
Measurable	*The suspension data eight weeks prior to the intervention are compared to data eight weeks after the intervention. We have the baseline data (fifteen suspensions total prior to the intervention: three suspension days per student for hands-on behavior) and a data collection system that will give us the end of the eight-week data.*
Attainable/ Achievable	*Note: Baseline data: three suspension days a week; total for four weeks prior is twelve suspensions.*
	We know our baseline data and believe with the implementation of an individualized intervention, a 50 percent decrease in suspension days after the four weeks is attainable.
Results-Oriented and Relevant	*Results-oriented: 50 percent decrease in suspension days compared to four weeks prior to beginning the individualized intervention suspension data.*
	Relevant: Research has found that students who were suspended and/or expelled— particularly those who were repeatedly disciplined—were more likely to be held back a grade or drop out of school than students not involved in the disciplinary system. When students were suspended or expelled, their likelihood of being involved in the juvenile justice system the subsequent year increased significantly.
	A Multi-Tiered System of Supports (MTSS) is a framework designed to provide tiered levels of support behaviorally and academically for all students. This includes teaching behavior similar to academics.
	Federal guidelines for schools to improve school climate and discipline include the following: creating positive climates and focus on prevention; developing clear, appropriate, and consistent expectations and consequences to address disruptive student behaviors (improve behavior, increase engagement, boost achievement); and ensuring fairness, equity, and continuous improvement.
	The Local Control and Accountability Plan (LCAP) highlights school climate and connectedness through a variety of factors, such as suspension and expulsion rates and other locally identified means.
Time-Bound	*By the end of the four weeks of intervention.*

PRACTICE: Use the blank template below with your PBIS Tier 3 sub-team to establish your Tier 3 intervention behavior goal.

SMART Goal Characteristics	Our Tier 3 Intervention Behavior Goal: Write your Tier 3 intervention behavior goal.
Strategic and Specific	Write the portion of your Tier 3 intervention behavior goal evidencing that it is strategic and specific.
Measurable	Write the portion of your Tier 3 intervention behavior goal evidencing that it is measurable.
Attainable/ Achievable	Explain why you believe your Tier 3 intervention behavior goal is attainable/ achievable.
Results-Oriented and Relevant	Write the portion of your Tier 3 intervention behavior goal evidencing that it is results-oriented and relevant.
Time-Bound	Write the portion of your Tier 3 intervention behavior goal evidencing that it is time-bound.

The final version of our Tier 3 intervention behavior SMART goal is . . .

_____

_____

_____

_____

_____

_____

_____

_____

_____

_____

_____

_____

Tier 3 Lessons Learned, Case Studies, and Bringing It All Together

This chapter begins with a few lessons learned from educators who have been trained in the development of our Positive Behavior Interventions and Supports (PBIS) Champion Model, representing more than five hundred schools. Next, we present three Tier 3 system and belief challenge case study examples from various educational settings (elementary school, middle school, high school, and an alternative education school). These Tier 3 implementation case studies focus on some of the challenges PBIS Champion Model Schools faced and the actions they took to move their individual systems to a Gold Level Tier 3 PBIS Champion Model. This chapter concludes with the opportunity for you to bring it all together and make sense of your current context and decide on your next course of action.

CASE STUDIES

As you read these case study challenges, reflect on the ABCs of developing a Gold Level Tier 3 PBIS Champion Model: Category A—Tier 3 Markers,

Category B—Tier 3 Characteristics, and Category C—Tier 3 Academic and Behavior Goals and the Work of the PBIS Tier 3 Sub-Team. These schools faced various challenges, and the leadership (administrative, teacher, and support staff) took specific actions to move each school from its current state to a more desired future—being recognized as a Tier 3 Gold Level PBIS Champion Model School. Consider the following lessons learned and focus questions as you read and reflect on each case study scenario:

Lessons Learned

- Administrator attendance at all PBIS Tier 3 sub-team meetings is essential. The PBIS Tier 3 sub-team members feel like their ideas are supported and heard.
- When alternative discipline is used appropriately and communication with staff about discipline decisions for students receiving Tier 3 interventions is timely, staff commitment is strengthened and sustained.
- When the PBIS Tier 3 sub-team holds itself accountable for its action plan steps, students and staff experience consistent implementation and follow-through.
- Feedback must be gathered on a regular, ongoing basis from stakeholders to maximize PBIS Tier 3 intervention implementation success and gain commitment from all.
- The allocation of protected time for the PBIS sub-team to meet at least weekly is essential for consistent implementation and staff messaging about progress.
- Establishing individualized intervention academic and behavior SMART (Strategic and Specific, Measurable, Attainable/Achievable, Results-Oriented and Relevant, and Time-Bound) goals is essential to the evaluation of a PBIS Tier 3 system and its effectiveness.
- Taking the time to educate stakeholders on Tier 3 interventions is key to implementation success.
- Funds should be allocated for Tier 3 resources and incentives.

Focus Questions

- What specific actions need to be taken in order to support the development of a strong PBIS Tier 3 foundation?
- What selected action(s) address Category A?
- What selected action(s) address Category B?
- What selected action(s) address Category C?
- What actions might you consider a *red flag* and indicate that something may need to be addressed?

TIER 3 IMPLEMENTATION
CASE STUDY CHALLENGE: BELIEF SYSTEM

School A administrators had a reputation for checking off all the boxes until they could kick out students at their school who were demonstrating Tier 3 behaviors. The belief system among the veteran staff was that students demonstrating Tier 3 behavioral support needs should be in an alternative school setting. In fact, the teachers would complain at every school board meeting about the handful of students at their school needing intensive supports. They would further defend their case by saying the teachers were getting burned out and were not safe around these students. In the past, the district leadership would give into the veteran teacher and leadership staff pressures without asking any questions; however, with the change in district leadership, the change in educational discipline laws, and the recent discipline disproportionality citation the district received for excessive exclusionary practices for students of color, the old belief system is no longer tolerated. However, the staff is continuing to put up a fight to kick students demonstrating Tier 3 behavioral needs out of their classrooms and school.

❧❧

What should this school do? Answer using the focus questions below as a guide:

What specific actions need to be taken in order to support the development of a strong PBIS Tier 3 foundation in this scenario?

_____

_____

_____

_____

_____

_____

What selected action(s) address Category A?

_____

_____

_____

(Continued)

(Continued)

What selected action(s) address Category B?

_____

_____

_____

What selected action(s) address Category C?

_____

_____

_____

What actions might you consider a *red flag* and indicate that something may need to be addressed?

_____

_____

_____

❧❧

TIER 3 IMPLEMENTATION CASE STUDY CHALLENGE: DISCONNECT BETWEEN GENERAL EDUCATION AND SPECIAL EDUCATION

There is a disconnect in School B between special education and general education tiered supports. This disconnect is causing confusion and inefficiency in how Tier 3 interventions are provided for both general education and special education students. Due to this divide, general education teachers do not feel as if they need to be part of any Tier 3 interventions for students receiving special education supports. They strongly believe the special education teacher, school psychologist, and special education aides should be in charge of the Tier 3 intervention development and implementation. Conversely, the special education teachers do not feel as if they should have a part in the development or implementation of general education Tier 3 intervention plans. As a result, there is not a consistent and clear Tier 3 system that includes the collaboration of both special education and general education. The administrators have no idea who is on a Tier 3 intervention plan and cannot speak to whether their plans are implemented with fidelity or effective.

What should this school do? Answer using the focus questions below as a guide:

What specific actions need to be taken in order to support the development of a strong PBIS Tier 3 foundation in this scenario?

_____

_____

_____

_____

_____

_____

What selected action(s) address Category A?

_____

_____

_____

What selected action(s) address Category B?

_____

_____

_____

What selected action(s) address Category C?

_____

_____

_____

What actions might you consider a *red flag* and indicate that something may need to be addressed?

_____

_____

_____

TIER 3 IMPLEMENTATION CASE STUDY CHALLENGE: COMPLICATED IMPLEMENTATION

School C has a handful of students receiving Tier 3 interventions. However, there is confusion as to what the plan looks like for each student. This confusion is leading to poor implementation and perception about the effectiveness of the plan in place. Stakeholders feel frustrated because they do not know what is expected of them with the plan. The plans given to them are extremely detailed and difficult to follow and ideally put in place.

What should this school do? Answer using the focus questions below as a guide:

What specific actions need to be taken in order to support the development of a strong PBIS Tier 3 foundation in this scenario?

_____

_____

_____

_____

_____

What selected action(s) address Category A?

_____

_____

What selected action(s) address Category B?

_____

_____

_____

What selected action(s) address Category C?

_____

_____

_____

What actions might you consider a *red flag* and indicate that something may need to be addressed?

_____

_____

_____

❧❧

BRINGING IT ALL TOGETHER

This book focuses on the building blocks of a Tier 3 Gold Level PBIS Champion Model, otherwise known as the ABCs of Tier 3. It was designed as an interactive guide to help you assess, learn, process, and action plan your next steps toward Gold Level implementation. Now let's bring it all together.

Fill in the summary sheet on the next page to help bring it all together.

Tier 3—Gold Level PBIS Champion Model Progress Summary Sheet		
Category A: Tier 3 Markers	**What is our score?**	**What is one action we will employ to make progress in this area? If the highest score was earned, *what will we do to sustain this high level?***
Marker 1: Establish and Operate an Effective PBIS Tier 3 Sub-Team		
Marker 2: Establish a Culture and Expectation for Supporting All Students		
Marker 3: Conduct a Tier 3 Resource Inventory		
Marker 4: Establish a Tier 3 Timely Response Plan		
Marker 5: Establish a Tier 3 Fidelity Check Process		
Category B: Tier 3 Characteristics	**What is our score?**	**What is one action we will employ to make progress in this area? If the highest score was earned, *what will we do to sustain this high level?***
Characteristic 1: Conduct a Student History Review		
Characteristic 2: Conduct an Environment Review		
Characteristic 3: Identify Function and Provide Replacement Skills		
Characteristic 4: Present Evidence of a Practical Plan/Schedule		
Characteristic 5: Plan for Progress Monitoring/Communication		
Category C: Tier 3 Academic and Behavior SMART Goals and the Work of the PBIS Tier 3 Sub-Team	**What is the final version of our Tier 3 intervention goals?** **What is one action we will employ to support progress toward achieving the goal?**	
Special Education Tier 3 Academic SMART Goal Special Education Tier 3 Behavior SMART Goal		
General Education Tier 3 Academic SMART Goal General Education Tier 3 Behavior SMART Goal		

Part III
What Next?

Next Steps and Tips for Success

Now that you have had a chance to digest the Tier 3 ABCs necessary to construct an effective Tier 3 behavior system at your school, it is time to practice. *So what is your role as a Tier 3 sub-team?* As a Tier 3 sub-team, you should meet at least once a week to address the intensive student challenges, both in general education and in special education based on your school's data. As a Tier 3 sub-team, your role is to develop, implement, and monitor Tier 3 interventions in a timely manner at your school.

Let's Practice: Read the scenarios and work through your first steps in developing a Tier 3 intervention that will address this student challenge. What resources are necessary to implement the Tier 3 intervention? How will you monitor and assess the Tier 3 intervention for effectiveness? Use the Tier 3 markers, Tier 3 characteristics, and Tier 3 SMART (Strategic and Specific, Measurable, Attainable/Achievable, Results-Oriented and Relevant, and Time-Bound) goals to help guide your next steps and actions accordingly.

Scenario 1

Fred refuses to complete classwork the majority of the school day. He only completes his math assignments; math is his favorite subject. He avoids all tasks that require him to read. When the teacher asks him to complete his work, he shuts down by pulling his hood over his head and eventually walks out of the classroom. When he is outside, he walks around and starts knocking on other classroom doors. He refuses to answer the adults trying to calm him down. It takes three or four adults and a couple hours each day to calm him down. This pattern of behavior has been going on for a month now. His parents are called daily for his behavior, but are frustrated with the school. The parents begin to blame the teachers and administrators in front of Fred every time they are asked to pick him up. The school team attempts a few Tier 2 behavior interventions, but Fred does not respond. The teachers and administrators are frustrated and feel defeated. Fred is falling behind and is avoiding anything academic. Fred is receiving special education services; however, he refuses to work with the special education teacher and support providers. Every time they attempt to work with him, he tells them to leave him alone and walks away from them. He has not met his academic goals and does not have any current behavior goals in place.

What are your first steps in developing a Tier 3 intervention to help address this student challenge?

_____

_____

_____

What resources are necessary to implement the Tier 3 intervention?

_____

_____

_____

How is the Tier 3 intervention monitored and assessed for effectiveness?

_____

_____

_____

Additional thoughts, discussion points, and possible actions:

_____

_____

_____

Scenario 2

Levi is a general education student who has received all of the Tier 2 interventions offered at the school, but continues to demonstrate the need for intensive behavioral supports. As soon as he is in an unstructured setting, he is either using inappropriate language with students, trying to instigate fights with students, or ignoring the adults at the school when he is given instruction. He tells the adults, "I don't have to listen to any of you," and walks away. Due to his behavior, Levi has all *F*s, is extremely behind, and is missing almost 80 percent of classroom instruction a week; he chooses to leave his classroom and even the school as he pleases—especially when he is asked to do anything he does not want to do. When he gets angry at either a student or an adult, he escalates to the point where it takes a team approach to calm him down and get him to a stable place. He has been known for climbing the baseball backstop and sitting up there for hours until he calms down. After hours of having his safety monitored and teachers attempting to get him down, he responds and ends up falling asleep in the administrator's office. This behavior continues daily for two weeks; the entire staff is at a loss and does not know how to respond or where even to start.

What are your first steps in developing a Tier 3 intervention to help address this student challenge?

_____

_____

_____

What resources are necessary to implement the Tier 3 intervention?

_____

_____

_____

(Continued)

(Continued)

How is the Tier 3 intervention monitored and assessed for effectiveness?

_____

_____

_____

Additional thoughts, discussion points, and possible actions:

_____

_____

_____

Scenario 3

Alfa is a very smart and capable student who is failing all of her classes. She has excessive tardies and absences in every period. She is a junior in high school and barely has a handful of freshman courses completed. She enjoys coming to school for the social aspect, but does not feel as if her classes are relevant to what she wants to do in life. It has gotten to the point where all the staff just let her come and go as she pleases because they do not want to get into a debate with her. She is known for being very argumentative and is able to cite human rights laws off the top of her head. Her foster parent is at the point where she has given up and is asking the school for additional support because she no longer knows what to do.

What are your first steps in developing a Tier 3 intervention to help address this student challenge?

_____

_____

_____

What resources are necessary to implement the Tier 3 intervention?

_____

_____

_____

How is the Tier 3 intervention monitored and assessed for effectiveness?

_____

_____

_____

Additional thoughts, discussion points, and possible actions:

_____

_____

_____

TIME TO PRACTICE

Identify a student needing a Tier 3 intervention at your school and write out a description of his or her behavior:

_____

_____

_____

_____

_____

What are your first steps in developing a Tier 3 intervention to help address this student challenge?

_____

_____

_____

_____

(Continued)

(Continued)

What resources are necessary to implement the Tier 3 intervention?

_____

_____

_____

_____

_____

How is the Tier 3 intervention monitored and assessed for effectiveness?

_____

_____

_____

_____

Additional thoughts, discussion points, and possible actions:

_____

_____

_____

_____

TIPS FOR SUCCESS

In this section, you will find tips from educators who are implementing the Positive Behavior Interventions and Supports (PBIS) Champion Model at the Gold Level:

- Keep the school's Tier 1 and Tier 2 academic and behavior foundation strong.
- Make implementation of an effective multi-tiered system a priority for the school.
- Ensure all administrators at the school are in full support of the implementation of Tier 3 interventions.
- Strengthen the collaboration between general education and special education staff.
- Be intentional about meeting weekly as a Tier 3 sub-team.
- Make sure your support staff (e.g., school psychologist) are on board for establishing effective Tier 3 systems.
- Create structures that support the implementation of Tier 3 interventions.
- Establish buy-in from all stakeholders.
- Collect and utilize data to make decisions and problem solve.
- Designate department or staff meeting time to update stakeholders on Tier 3 interventions.
- Be practical but intentional in implementation of Tier 3 interventions.
- Persevere, even if it gets frustrating.
- Be resilient to setbacks and naysayers.
- Keep your focus on what is best for students.

The most impactful tip we can give you is to believe that what you are doing will help students needing intensive individualized supports to access their education. Understanding your purpose to make an impact on a student's life is critical. You may not see the fruits of your labor initially, but matching the correct intervention with the student, establishing relationships, and following the actions in this book will pay off in the end.

Index

Figures are indicated by f following the page number.

CORWIN

A SAGE Publishing Company

Helping educators make the greatest impact

CORWIN HAS ONE MISSION: to enhance education through intentional professional learning.

We build long-term relationships with our authors, educators, clients, and associations who partner with us to develop and continuously improve the best evidence-based practices that establish and support lifelong learning.

Solutions you want. Experts you trust. Results you need.